BOOKS BY MARY CABLE

The Blizzard of '88   1988

Top Drawer:
American High Society from the Gilded Age
to the Roaring Twenties   1984

Avery's Knot (a novel)   1981

Lost New Orleans   1980

The Little Darlings:
A History of Child-Rearing in America   1975

El Escorial   1971

Black Odyssey:
The Case of the Slaveship Amistad   1971

The Avenue of the Presidents   1969

American Manners and Morals   1969

Dream Castles   1966

The
BLIZZARD of '88

The
BLIZZARD of '88

MARY CABLE

NEW YORK *Atheneum* 1988

To

my brother, LARRY PRATT,

and his wife, EMILY,

with much love

Library of Congress Cataloging-in-Publication Data
Cable, Mary.
The blizzard of '88.
1. Blizzards—Northeastern States.   2. Northeastern
States—History.   I. Title.
QC929.S7C25   1988   551.5′55′0974   87-14570
ISBN 0-689-11591-1

Atheneum
Macmillan Publishing Company
866 Third Avenue, New York, N.Y. 10022
Collier Macmillan Canada, Inc.

Macmillan books are available at special discounts for bulk purchases
for sales promotions, premiums, fund-raising, or education use.
For details, contact:

Special Sales Director
Macmillan Publishing Company
866 Third Avenue
New York, N.Y. 10022

10 9 8 7 6 5 4 3 2 1

PRINTED IN THE UNITED STATES OF AMERICA

Contents

Acknowledgments

Grateful thanks are due, first of all, to my husband, Arthur G. Cable, Jr., for his patience, helpfulness, and good cheer. The Ragdale Foundation and the Virginia Center for the Creative Arts provided splendid working conditions. And the following people gave me valuable suggestions, corrections, and much-appreciated help of various kinds:

Oliver Jensen; David McCullough; Sheila Pellegrini; Governor Michael Castle, of Delaware, and, in Lewes, Delaware, Hazel Brittingham and Henry Marshall; David M. Ludlum, of the American Weather History Center; John A. Gable, of the Theodore Roosevelt Association; Thomas J. Dunnings and Mariam Touba of the New-York Historical Society; Madeline Winter, of the Berkshire *Eagle*, Pittsfield, Massachusetts; Millie Daghli, of AT & T; Marjorie H. Ciarlante and Lee Johnson, of the National Archives; Virginia Wood, of the Library of Congress; Lucinda Birke-Pile, of the New Haven Historical Society; Terry Ariano, of the Museum of the City of New York; Lincoln Paine, of the National Maritime Historical Society; and James H. Driscoll, of the Society of the Silurians.

Introduction

ON MONDAY, MARCH 12, 1888, a tremendous blizzard struck the eastern seaboard of the United States, causing havoc from Maryland to Maine. Early in the storm, all seventy-four telegraph wires between Washington and Baltimore blew down, and by the end of Monday almost every other wire in the East was down, too. The Albany *Journal*, addressing those few citizens who might be reading it, forlornly noted, "New York is as remote from us as Tokio."

Hundreds of trains were stalled for days, immobilized by twenty- and thirty-foot snow drifts. In the cities, public transportation ceased, businessmen could do no business, coal supplies dwindled, and babies were crying for milk. At sea, the storm was a hurricane, with winds up to ninety miles an hour. Waves three stories high pounded the rocks of New England and crashed across the beaches of Long Island, New Jersey, and Delaware. One hundred and ninety-eight ships were either sunk, damaged, or driven ashore, and nearly a hundred seamen died. On land, the death toll came to more than three hundred, by accident, freezing, or storm-caused illness.

To rank as a true blizzard, a storm must combine heavy snowfall, bitter cold, and a fierce wind that mingles the snow in the air with the snow on the ground, whirling it madly about until anyone in its midst can see almost nothing else. Such snow is not soft and pretty, but consists of tiny, sharp particles of flying ice that sting and cut. And all this continues without much surcease for two to three days.

The Blizzard of '88, as this storm has come to be known, was a true blizzard in all respects, an uncommon occurrence on the east coast. That same year, several blizzards struck the west, one in the Dakotas and the others sweeping through southwestern range country and destroying thousands of cattle; but as far as easterners were concerned, their blizzard was *the* Blizzard of '88. A formidable storm, indeed. Still, there have been others in the East, before and since, and one has to ask what it was about this particular one that has made it a folk memory, ranking with such famous disasters as the Johnstown Flood and the sinking of the *Titanic*. For decades, newspapers never failed to note its anniversary, and all subsequent storms were inevitably compared to it. In 1929, the Society of Blizzard Men was formed in New York, and thousands who had lived through the great storm became members, so that they could attend the annual luncheon and exchange memories. The Society of Blizzard Men (later invaded by Blizzard Ladies) continued until the last few members had either died or were too feeble to attend a lunch.

One member, who, in 1888, had been a carpet salesman in Manhattan, looked back fifty years later and pondered the reasons for the blizzard's powerful impact: "The uncertainty that all felt," he wrote, "the loss of life, the fear of fire, the hardships that many must suffer, no communication with the

United States . . . the sparse news seeping through, though not knowing whether true or not, the low temperature, a terrific wind and snowdrifts and snowfall all contributed to an almost paralyzing anxiety."

In 1888, such widespread anxiety had not been experienced since the Civil War. A whole generation had grown up since then, and the cheerful, forward-looking time to which 1888 belonged has come to be called the Age of Confidence. People were anxious about their individual problems, of course, but they felt no general, ongoing apprehension about overwhelming events beyond their control. That kind of distress was still another half-century or more in the future.

The 1880s had brought astonishing new inventions and discoveries that were already benefiting the rich and promising to ease and brighten life for everyone. The great eastern cities now had telephones, steam-heated buildings (a few hundred of each), and electric lights (on main streets and in wealthy households). In New York City, anyone with five cents could ride on the elevated railroads, which, by 1888, had been in service for about nine years; and all but the very poor were blessed with indoor plumbing. The decade had brought major medical breakthroughs, such as antiseptic surgery, local anesthesia, and antirabies vaccine, to say nothing of such pleasing amenities as flatirons, fountain pens, and adding machines. Improvements to earlier technology kept coming as well: the modern bicycle (1884), the alternating-current transformer (1885), the Kodak camera (1888), and the electric trolley (not quite ready in 1888 but on its way).

On the national scene, there seemed nothing much to worry about. The deep wounds left by the Civil War were slowly healing, and no other wars appeared imminent. In the West, the last defiant Apaches had been removed to detention camps in Florida, and the frontier was now secure for settlers. By and large, the nation looked safe, sober, and promising, at least to its ruling middle class, a group that tended to be daring in technological advance and high-flying in business, yet conservative politically and glad to have a conservative president, Grover Cleveland. All in all, most Americans in 1888 felt tranquil and hopeful. Their world looked fine and likely to get better. And, in the face of recent medical miracles, even death seemed to have moved back a little.

People who lived in the eastern states were apt to be more smug and self-satisfied than westerners, whom they often looked down upon as rough innocents. Most arrogant of all were the New Yorkers, who saw themselves as living at the forefront of civilization. If there had been T-shirts a hundred years ago, they might have read as some do today: "When you leave New York, you ain't goin' nowhere."

Then, suddenly, into that city of technological marvels came the Blizzard of '88 and turned it upside down. Not that other parts of the northeast did not suffer acutely; but in smaller places and in the country, people were still living a simpler life and had time-honored ways of dealing with storms. They stayed home and turned to supplies laid in during the previous autumn; they didn't miss electricity, or running water, or telephones because they weren't used to them; nor did they look to anyone but themselves and their neighbors to plow the roads. If no help appeared for days, they could wait. They were on an ancient time schedule, while New York had already anticipated the twentieth century.

And so the tale of the blizzard keeps leading back to New York City, chiefly because of the striking contrast between its seeming strength and its real fragility. "Society cannot bear anarchy," Barbara Tuchman write in *A Distant Mirror*. The Blizzard of '88 swept down on a self-satisfied society and showed it what anarchy might look like.

4

SATURDAY, MARCH 10

Saturday,
March 10

SATURDAY, MARCH 10, 1888, was a bright springlike day in all the northeast states, with temperatures in the fifties or higher and a gentle south wind. Along the Chesapeake Bay, fishing boats, especially oystermen and crabbers, were everywhere on the placid blue water. In the cities, from Baltimore to Boston, the gentle Italian love music of organ-grinders drifted incongruously above the clatter of American streets. At the offices of the Wilmington, Delaware, newspaper, *Every Evening*, a man named John Cooper rushed in to inform the editors that his cherry tree, as usual, was about to produce the region's first cherry blossoms. The tree grew close to Mr. Cooper's chimney and, encouraged by both the sun and the hot bricks, annually outdid ordinary cherry trees.

In New York City that morning, the shopping streets of Manhattan below 23rd Street were thronged with bargain hunters, eager for end-of-winter sales. On Grand Street, where the stores were big and low-priced, Ridley's, a drygoods store, was offering twelve hundred drastically reduced snow shovels; but this was hardly a good day to sell snow shovels, and the manager was wondering where he would store them over the summer.

The weather was perfect for sightseeing. Out-of-town visitors and New Yorkers alike thronged to Central Park to enjoy the zoo, or took a Fifth Avenue stage all the way up to 82nd Street to have a look through the small but flourishing Metropolitan Museum of Art, and then strolled back down the avenue past the mansarded and turreted mansions of the very rich. Others rode elevated railway trains all the way down to the tip of Manhattan and then boarded ferries for Bedloe's Island, where the city's latest wonder, the Statue of Liberty, had been open to the public since the previous April. Still others, following the advice of guidebooks, stopped in at 120 Broadway, the Equitable Life Assurance Building, to marvel at the view from the tower and to gawk at the operations of the New York Weather Station, which was housed there.

When the United States Weather Service was established by Congress in 1870, the tower of the then brand-new seven-story Equitable Building was chosen for the New York station because it was the highest point in the city, 150 feet above the ground, and easily accessible by means of the first hydraulic elevators in the world. Now, in 1888, there were a few higher buildings, but the Equitable had added an eighth story and raised its tower to 172 feet. (Tourists were also impressed by its ground-floor shopping arcade, European-style courtyard with fountains and greenery, and flush toilets on every floor.) Moving slowly but inexorably upward, the hydraulic elevators delivered visitors to the top of the tower, where (as one guidebook put it) one could "look down from this dizzying height upon the marvelous stretch of scenery taking in the Narrows, Staten Island, the North and the East River, and the major portion of New York and Brooklyn." One could also walk out on the roof

8

to examine the instruments that measured humidity, rain, wind, and temperature and, from a discreet distance, observe the Weather Service personnel, who were noncommissioned officers and enlisted men in the Army Signal Corps.

One staff member, whom visitors often asked to have pointed out, was Sergeant Francis Long, known to the general public because his colorful career had been the subject of several newspaper stories. A teenage immigrant from Germany in the late 1860s, he had joined the Army of the West and had survived, with minor scratches, some ten years of Indian fighting. June 26, 1876, had found his company heading for the Little Big Horn River, where General Custer intended to subdue the Sioux and their allies. Luckily for Long, he was not with Custer but with General Terry, some twenty miles distant, when Custer, fourteen officers, and two hundred and fifty enlisted men were killed. Long was fond of telling friends that the day after he had been first on the battlefield, and that it was he who had found the bodies of Custer and some of his officers, but history has not documented this claim.

In 1881, he had volunteered as cook for an Arctic expedition under General Adolphus W. Greely. Through a series of misadventures and mistakes, Greely's party became lost and marooned. A ship sent to look for them in 1882 failed to find them, and it was not until June 1884 that they were finally rescued. By that time, the party had dwindled to six survivors, all within a few days of death from starvation. Lucky again: Sergeant Long was one of the six.

This time his narrow escape made him something of a celebrity. The newspapers had been keeping the Greely expedition in the public mind, and when Long and a couple of the other survivors recovered their strength, they toured on the lecture circuit. At each stop, Long had proven a favorite. He was a big, genial, red-haired man, full of jokes, and a good storyteller.

9

On the money earned from the lecture tour, he had married and settled in Brooklyn. General Greely (who had survived as well) had become chief of the Weather Service, and he was glad to give Long his present good job and the chance to lead a quiet, safe life poring over weather charts. Long was good at it and probably enjoyed his celebrity, but sitting at a desk all day sometimes made him restless and gloomy. It was said that he drank too much. Here in Manhattan he may sometimes have found it hard to realize that he had ever galloped after Indians on the plains of the Dakotas or hunted polar bears at the North Pole.

On that sunny Saturday, he certainly would not have believed that another death-defying adventure was only two days away.

Sergeant Long's malaise was at least somewhat relieved by the splendid view from the window beside his desk. Spread out before him was lower Manhattan, the commercial center of the western hemisphere: markets, shops, hotels, office buildings, abattoirs, docks, and the decaying mansions of the previous century now turned into slums. The streets were in constant frantic motion with wagons, horsecars, cabs, carriages, and pedestrians. In the last few years, huge utility poles had sprouted in these streets, towering over them and strung with so many telegraph, telephone, and electric wires as to actually cut off a good deal of daylight. Also dimming several main thorough-fares were the great iron trestles of the elevated railroads, where trains rattled and banged along, pulled by scaled-down steam locomotives. To the north stretched the rest of Manhattan Island, the nearer part solidly built up with block after block of brownstone houses, the more distant areas a haphazard mélange of isolated rows of new brownstones, interspersed by old farm-houses, squatters' shanties, empty lots, woods, and cow pastures.

Flowing along on each side of the island were the rivers—or so-called rivers: the East River is really a tidal inlet; and the Hudson, or North, River is really a fjord. Both were lively with side-wheel ferryboats thrashing back and forth, arriving and departing steamers, and all manner of sailing ships, which made up more than half the traffic. On any day along the wharves, one could see square-rigged sailing ships, fishing schooners, cargo schooners, yachts, barks, brigantines, oyster sloops, and sailing lighters. There were also a few Erie canal boats—anachronisms in 1888, but still in service.

Saturday was the busiest day for oceangoing vessels. On that particular Saturday, eight transatlantic liners left their piers and steamed off down the bay, and nine pilot schooners set sail in search of incoming ships that needed shepherding into harbor. Nineteen were due that weekend.

On board the pilotboat *Caldwell F. Colt* was a young New York *World* reporter named William O. Inglis, assigned to do a feature story on the life of harbor pilots. Inglis was twenty-six years old and had only just started at the *World* after five years at the *Herald.* Anxious to make a good impression, he had not mentioned to his new editor that even a ferry ride made him queasy. Instead, taking advantage of the fine weather, he had made arrangements to go to sea with number 13 pilot boat, the *Colt.*

As they sailed down the bay, Inglis, in an effort to forget the uneasy stirrings inside him, took out his notebook and began interviewing the pilots. He learned that the *Colt* was an eighty-five-foot, two-masted schooner, weighing 61.4 tons and carrying five pilots, a boatkeeper, a steward, and four men before the mast. The number 1 pilot, James Fairgreaves, was in command, the captain having stayed ashore in order to give Inglis his berth. Fairgreaves was an old hand in the business—which, until steam replaced the pilots' sails after 1900, was a rough, tough way of making a living. The pilots were in competition with each other, and when large ships were expected, numerous pilot boats set off full tilt down the bay, bound for the coastal waters beyond Sandy Hook. Today, nine of them were racing to intercept the New York–bound vessels.

Outside Sandy Hook the pilots would wait for a glimpse of smoke on the horizon, and then pile on sail to see which would be first to come up on the incoming vessel's lee side. American ships, if they chose, could decline a pilot, but foreign ships were obliged to take one aboard. The larger the vessel, the higher the fee. Sometimes the scramble to corral a remunerative client was so reckless as to result in collision and loss of life. There was also a danger that the pilot schooner would be run down by the larger vessel. That had happened more than once while the pilot was being put aboard.

To become a licensed pilot took nine years, and the money was never very good. The fast little schooners were expensive to build and to care for. Each one carried up to six pilots, and since they had to take turns, some pilots always came back to port without having made a nickel. The whole procedure was wasteful, inefficient, and dangerous, but the pilots wanted it no other way. When, in the late 1890s, laws were passed to end the racing, many of the old hands were so indignant that they retired from the profession.

Halfway down the bay that Saturday afternoon, the *Colt* passed the *Enchantress,* the oldest pilot schooner in the service. She was, perhaps, not very fast, but she was reliable: pilots thought well of *Enchantress.* Acting captain Fairgreaves told Inglis about her as they passed, and later called his attention to a handsome new yacht, the *Cythera,* out of the Seawanhaka Corinthian Yacht Club at Oyster Bay and bound for the Caribbean on her maiden voyage. The pilots admired her lines but muttered something about fancy landlubbers aboard. The owner and skipper, W. W. Stewart, was a Long Island socialite who had just graduated from a course in yachtsmanship. Three other gentlemen on board were experienced yachtsmen. Also aboard were a cook, a steward, and a hired crew of four. The craft, as she overtook the *Colt,* was being handled flawlessly, and she sped past every other sailing vessel in sight.

Inglis, taking note of a slight increase in the gentle roll of the ship, watched the *Cythera* as she sliced through the waters of the Narrows and disappeared over the horizon. Then he decided to take to his berth for a while. As he wrote later, his "tired and vibrating diaphragm" needed a rest.

The New York Weather Station staff worked until midnight on Saturdays and most had Sundays off until 5 P.M. Three times a day, all 154 stations sent telegraphed reports to Washington headquarters. After analyzing the data, Washington then sent to each station a report on weather that might affect its region. That morning, New York had learned that an enormous area of low pressure—a trough—stretching north–south from Canada to the Gulf Coast, was heading eastward at a rapid rate. Low-pressure centers—cyclones—were centered near Green Bay, Wisconsin, and over St. Louis, Missouri. A midday report said that the southern cyclone had moved to the southeast, bringing heavy rain to Georgia and Florida, and that rain or snow was falling all the way north to Michigan.

None of this seemed cause for alarm in New York, however, and Sergeant Long, with several cronies, went out about six o'clock and spent the allotted forty-five-minute supper hour over a hefty meal. A good restaurant nearby served hearty suppers: chops, sausage, bacon, grilled kidneys, and baked potatoes; and for dessert, a "slip-on," which was hot mince pie drenched with Welsh rarebit.

In the early evening, the streets were teeming with homeward-bound working people, all hurrying pell-mell for ferries, horse-cars, commuter trains, cablecars across the Great Bridge to Brooklyn, or the els, which had, during the 1880s, revolutionized many lives by making it possible to work downtown and live in upper Manhattan or the Bronx. But the els were already inadequate for the number of people they had to carry.

On that particular Saturday, the crowds were greater than usual because the Barnum and Bailey Circus had come to town and its grand preopening parade was causing traffic jams. Along its route, thousands blocked the sidewalks and gathered at upper-story windows. "The Elevated Railroad had to turn away passengers," reported the *Herald* next day. "The police were helpless for they had no heart to club anyone."

The parade began at dusk at Madison Square Garden. Lit by volunteer torchbearers (each rewarded with a free circus ticket), it proceeded down Broadway as far as Grand Street, and then returned uptown by a roundabout West Side route, ending where it had started, at Madison Avenue and 26th Street. The torchbearers dropped away during the long, tiring march but were present in force at the end, in order to claim their tickets.

After the torchbearers came a golden chariot filled with acrobats and bareback riders. It was followed by a military band in uniforms of orange and gold, and, close behind, elaborate animal cages on wheels, drawn by teams of horses, and carrying lions, tigers, sea lions, wolves, hyenas, bears, leopards, and monkeys—"the finest since Noah"—as Barnum was advertising them. A team of camels pulled a chariot whose passengers were Mother Goose and Cinderella. And still another chariot, this one full of clowns, was pulled by two young elephants. (Jumbo, "world's largest elephant"—probably the most popular ever of Barnum's attractions—had been killed the year before in a train accident.)

Not the least attraction was P. T. Barnum himself, a peppy old gentleman of seventy-seven. That evening, he was waiting at the Metropolitan Hotel on Broadway at Prince Street to review the parade from a balcony. Then, suddenly, an incident occurred that only Barnum, with his quick wit and skill, could have handled with equanimity. A fire broke out in a building opposite the hotel and threatened to disrupt the proceedings entirely, as fire engines raced across the parade route.

"Let the building go, I'll pay for it," cried Barnum, first making sure a reporter was listening. "I won't have this great multitude disappointed."

The police managed to reroute the parade to the next block, and Barnum, pursuing it in a cab, became part of it.

On Grand Street, below the elevated tracks, the young elephants pulling the clowns' chariot took fright when a train rumbled by over their heads. They broke into a run, dragging the chariot onto a sidewalk. Tragedy threatened, but the trainers controlled their charges before anyone got hurt.

The parade was over and the streets empty by the time the Weather Station staff was preparing its "indications" (as forecasts were then called) for the next day, Sunday, March 11. The evening report from Washington had stated that the low-pressure trough was now approaching the Appalachians. The cyclone in Wisconsin had phased out, and the southern one was now heading in a direction that would take it out to sea near Cape Hatteras. Streams of very cold Canadian air were flowing into Newfoundland and the New England states, where they would be coming up against a stalled, or very slow-moving, area of high pressure.

Based on this information, the indications sent out to the newspapers (and to private subscribers, who paid to receive weather reports by telegram) read:

For Maine, New Hampshire, Vermont, Massachusetts, Rhode Island, Connecticut, eastern New York, eastern Pennsylvania, and New Jersey, fresh to brisk southeasterly winds, slightly warmer, fair weather, followed by rain.
For the District of Columbia, Maryland, Delaware, and Virginia, fresh to brisk southeasterly winds, slightly warmer, threatening weather and rain.

The Weather Service claimed to be right about 82 percent of the time. This may have been true in some parts of the country—but not in the northeast, where conditions at sea had a strong influence and were not, at that time, predictable. Wireless communication with ships had not yet been invented and would not come into general use until after 1900. The jet stream was not yet understood, nor was it possible to know what was going on at very high altitudes.

However, on that evening, if any of the staff of the New York Station saw an ominous sign in the indications, there is no record of it.

As he put on his coat to go home, Sergeant Long looked out of the east window and saw a moonless night, with many bright stars shining down on Brooklyn and its bridge. Of all the technological triumphs of the 1880s, the Great Bridge was perhaps the most impressive, at least to New Yorkers and Brooklynites. Visible from miles around, it was a magnificent symbol: a bridge to a future of scientific marvels, and to a safe and comfortable world where everything would work perfectly.

SUNDAY,
MARCH 11

Sunday, March 11

PRESIDENT AND MRS. CLEVELAND, spending the weekend at their country place near Washington, were detained indoors during most of Sunday because of heavy rain. By evening, temperatures were dropping and winds rising, and the rain turned to snow. In the middle of the night, the Clevelands were awakened by a crash outside their window, and next day they were dismayed to find that a favorite elm had gone down. The president was perhaps even more dismayed when he found that all the telegraph wires were down as well and that Washington was out of contact with most of the nation.

During the seventeen hours when the Weather Service was observing the sabbath, the weather was undergoing rapid changes. The cyclone near Cape Hatteras passed out to sea as expected, but instead of continuing on a northeasterly course, which would have taken it into the Atlantic east of Nantucket, it suddenly shifted and headed directly north. As it traveled, it picked up quantities of warm, moist ocean air, which caused enormous turbulence on encountering the cold air of the cyclone. Meantime, the eastward-moving low-pressure trough was passing quickly over the Appalachians.

Along the coast, skippers observed the falling barometer and put into port if they could. At the mouth of the Delaware Bay, the little town of Lewes had a newly improved breakwater, capable of sheltering dozens of ships and small craft. Without it, this port would have been of little use to the heavy traffic of commercial shipping that traveled that coast. The bay offers no natural shelter. Sudden storms blow directly on anchored or moving ships and conditions can become dangerous in a few minutes. In winter, ice floats down the river, clogging the long, winding channel. Many ships have been lost in these waters, including the famous *DeBraak,* a reputedly gold-laden Dutch privateer sunk in 1798 by one of those sudden storms, and located again in 1984.

Despite its hazards, Lewes was a much-frequented port of call for ships on the middle of Atlantic coast. The Pennsylvania Railroad maintained a fifteen-hundred-foot pier inside the breakwater, for transshipping cargoes. And because Lewes is about halfway between Florida and New England, captains found it convenient to put in there and pick up orders from their owners, as well as mail and supplies.

In summertime, middle-class families came to Lewes to enjoy the sea air, the sandy beaches, and the pretty seventeenth-century town. In winter, Lewes had few visitors besides seamen, but on this particular Sunday a young divinity school student from Princeton, John H. Marshall, was there to preach at the Presbyterian church. After the service, the young man and his host, the local minister, dined and then went for a walk. A mild rain was falling and the sea was gray and restless. Sailors from the anchored ships were wandering about disconsolately, and those from European countries were cursing the American Sunday blue laws. Nothing to do, nothing to drink.

After an evening service, Marshall walked back to the minister's house, this time in a harder rain and a gusty southeast wind, and went to sleep to the sound of surf, which had scarcely been noticeable the previous night. About midnight, he was awakened from a sound sleep by shouts in the street outside. The night was inky dark, except for thick flakes of snow flying past his window.

"To the pier!" voices were shouting. "Hurry! To the pier!"

Marshall and his host dressed quickly and hurried with many other townsmen along the beach road that led to the long wooden pier inside the breakwater. The wind was blowing so hard that Marshall could hardly keep his footing, and it was some time before he could get anyone to stop and explain what seemed to him sheer chaos. Slicker-clad figures rushed past, carrying lanterns that bobbed wildly. At the pier, these flickering lights fell upon a terrifying scene of heaving, listing ships, dashing waves, and sails flapping out of control. Men were dragging heavy coils of rope to the side of the pier, while over the loud surf came frantic calls for help.

The wind, which had blown all day from the southeast, moderate to fresh, had very suddenly veered around to the north and then to the northwest, and was now shrieking a violent gale. The thirty-five ships anchored in the breakwater had been caught unprepared. Almost before any seaman could respond to "All hands on deck!" anchor chains broke, masts snapped, and steamships and schooners and tugs alike were driven into one another. Several went crashing into the long wooden pier, and one, the tug *Lizzie V. Crawford*, rammed straight through it, snapping the heavy timbers. The tremendous surf then drove her onto the beach. Another tug, the

George Simpson, whose captain had his wife aboard, collided with the pier and then, with engines in reverse, backed into a steamship, the *Tamesei*. Both vessels began to sink. To their rescue came another tug, appropriately named *Protector*. Despite the great danger of further collision, a rope was hauled aboard the *Simpson* and reeled in until the two tugs were touching. Most of the *Simpson*'s crew were able to jump to the rescuer's deck. The captain's wife, waiting intrepidly for a moment when the immense waves would bring the two decks relatively even, jumped and was caught by the *Protector*'s captain.

The bow of the *Simpson* had struck the *Tamesei* amidships, and from the two holds came the sound dreaded by all seamen: the hissing of steam as seawater rushed aboard and flooded the engines. Both vessels sank rapidly, and the *Simpson*'s mate and one crewman found themselves struggling for their lives in the frigid sea. They were lucky enough to be pulled onto the pilings of the broken pier by some of the *Tamesei*'s crew, who had taken refuge there. Later in the night, still another vessel crashed into the pier, and her captain and some of her crew joined the other castaways. In all, that night, eleven men were cast away on the shaky outer end of the pier.

When daylight dawned, the pier and the breakwater (as Marshall wrote later) "presented a wild sight." The pier had been severed in three places, and it was clear that there was no way for the hapless men at the far end of it to get themselves ashore. Violent waves would prevent an easy rescue by boat, and their precarious perch might collapse at any moment. All the men were soaked to the skin, and their clothing had frozen, so that to those on shore they looked like figures carved in ice. They were nearly as motionless, because they dared not walk up and down or even stamp their feet to keep warm, lest their unreliable refuge collapse. The distance between them and the shore was five hundred yards, well within the reach of a breeches buoy; but to use one was impossible because nothing out there would hold a rope. Rescue by boat was the only possibility: a job for the professionals from the lifesaving station, with their self-bailing surfboat. But the crews of both the Lewes and the Cape Henlopen stations were busy down the shore a mile or two, where at least fourteen schooners and several steam freighters had gone aground.

John Marshall, well soaked and with his face cut by flying sand, sadly retraced his steps to the minister's house, and packed his bag. It is possible that he felt a number of unfamiliar emotions: frustration, fear, uselessness, sorrow, and general apprehension. He was not particularly robust and he had no clothes for a storm. He was, in fact, in the way. He therefore went to the Philadelphia, Wilmington and Baltimore railroad depot, and boarded a train (two cars) to return to Princeton, a less ebullient but perhaps wiser divinity student. The train tottered a few miles down the track and then stuck fast in a snowdrift as high as the roof of the cars. There it remained, with Marshall, four other passengers, and the crew, until Wednesday.

Meanwhile, down the beach, the lifesaving crews were hard at work.* As dawn broke on Monday, it was possible to perceive in the breakers just offshore the looming shapes of vessels gone aground. One was the *Alice H. Belden,* from Portland, Connecticut, stuck fast about two hundred yards out. Waves were breaking over her decks, and her crew could be faintly made out, clinging to the rigging. The lifesavers fired a line that reached her deck, but just as the captain caught hold of it, the wind tore it away. The next landed across the jibboom, but the waves were breaking so heavily that those on board dared not leave the rigging

---

*Official lifesaving stations had been in existence on this dangerous coast only since 1871. They were under the aegis of the Department of Commerce, and remained so until 1912, when they were transferred to the Coast Guard. Every year they earned their keep many times over in lives and ships saved.

to secure it, and it soon washed off. Before the lifesavers could ready another line, a new squall set in and the schooner disappeared from their sight in whirling snow. Other stranded schooners were nearer shore, so a decision was made to rescue those crews first, by surfboat.

Later in the day, attention was returned to the *Belden*. This time a surfboat was successfully launched through the breakers, and, by rowing strenuously and dropping anchor when they had to rest, the rescuers brought their craft alongside the sinking schooner. Two of those in the rigging had by this time weakened and fallen to their deaths in the mountainous seas. The rest were brought ashore, after clinging aloft for twelve hours. All were nearly dead from frostbite and exposure, as were three of their rescuers. But all eventually recovered, and their captain wrote a letter of thanks to the superintendent of Lifesaving Stations in Washington.

Not until nearly dusk was the exhausted crew of the Lewes Lifesaving Station able to turn its attention to the marooned seamen on the broken pier. At considerable danger to themselves, they tied their gun to the shore side of the broken pier and fired a line to the castaways. A hawser, attached to a surfboat, followed the line, and by this means the men on the pier hauled the boat alongside, got into it, and were pulled ashore. In all, forty people were rescued that day by the two local stations, and many others were saved by stations all the way from Maine to Cape Hatteras.

At the Lewes hospital, seventeen seamen were treated. One had gone out of his mind, one had a rupture caused by hard rowing, others were expected to be maimed for life, and nearly all were frostbitten. Those who had spent hours in the rigging of sinking ships had deep seams and cracks in their hands, and feet that were twisted out of shape.

At the breakwater alone, financial losses came to more than

$300,000, including $35,000 for the steamer *Tamesei*, and $50,000 for the pier.

From New Jersey north through New England, most of Sunday, March 11, was overcast but not stormy. The weather had lost the springlike buoyancy of Saturday, but there was nothing about it to prompt changes in the usual routine of American Sundays. In the 1880s, the powerful influence of the Puritan fathers, though waning, was still felt, particularly in New England and even among people whose ancestors had never been Puritans. Sunday was a day for religion, rest, and family but not for frivolity. Parents and children put on their best clothes and went to church, then came home and sat down to the best meal of the week, which would center around a roast and a pie. A family walk might follow. No work was to be done (except, of course, by women and servants, preparing and cleaning up the dinner), and old-fashioned parents forbade games. Reading was permitted, as long as it was of an edifying nature: no novels, no children's stories, no newspapers. In Boston, the *Transcript* was so confident that its readers would reject it on the Lord's Day that it offered no Sunday edition.

Sunday afternoons and evenings were also times for getting together with close relatives, and at twilight it was traditional to gather around the piano or parlor organ for a hymn-sing. Such homey customs suited life in country towns and villages, where aunts, uncles, and grandparents usually lived close enough for frequent visits. Country people who moved to the city, as many did in the 1880s, brought their customs with them and were willing to travel miles by horsecar or elevated railroad if relatives were anywhere within reach.

New immigrants, especially those from Catholic countries, sometimes had a hard time getting used to the American Sunday. Most were accustomed to church in the morning, although they felt no Puritan urgency to get there every week. But after church, they expected to find shops open and to spend social afternoons in beer gardens or other convivial places that served light refreshments and provided music. It seemed appalling to them to find shops, saloons, concert halls, theaters, and even merry-go-rounds all firmly locked up on Sundays.

Abram Hewitt, New York's reform mayor elected in 1886, thought such strict laws needed revision. Impoverished immigrants slaved all week at the lowest kind of work and then went home to quarters that were, at best, dreary and, at worst, airless and crowded. They badly needed pleasant places to go on their one day off, places where they could hear music, see friends, and sip a glass of wine or beer without being judged depraved. Hewitt wanted respectable places of that nature to have Sunday licenses; but there he came up against the powerful temperance movement.

When Hewitt came to office, he found that many saloons quietly did business on Sundays because their owners were paying off the police. His ingenious solution was to enforce the closing of all of them. The result was such a furor in the powerful Irish and German wards of the city that the legislature hastily empowered him to grant certain carefully selected Sunday licenses. In this way, evil dives were closed down and blameless cafés, clubs, and music halls stayed open.

And so it happened that many New Yorkers were out late that Sunday evening and became the first to know about the storm. Two young German-Americans in Brooklyn, returning two young ladies to their homes after an evening at the *Sängerbundhalle,* found the gutters overflowing in a torrential rain. They had to carry the girls on their backs, which seemed at first hilarious and then less so, as sleet began to fall and the sidewalk turned to ice.

Another young man who lived below Grand Street and had been calling on his sweetheart uptown, arrived home very late, his hat blown away and his best clothes ruined in the sudden onslaught of hail and sleet. As he reached his block, he was astonished to see the wind suddenly seize the front steps of an old frame house and hurtle them down the street.

He had been lucky enough to find a newsboy selling early morning editions of the *Herald*. As soon as he was inside his front door, he turned with curiosity to the weather forecast:

In this city and suburban districts today colder, partly cloudy to fair weather and brisk to fresh westerly to northwesterly winds will probably prevail followed by clear conditions.

Relieved, but still not entirely reassured, the young man got out of his wet clothes, and used the newspaper to help start a fire in the grate.

MONDAY, MARCH 12

1

Blizzard Monday

NEW YORKERS who had gone to bed on Sunday evening to the sound of rain were startled on Monday morning to find snow sifting in through cracks around their windows and piling up in front of their doors so fast that even those who left home at dawn had to dig their way out. The wind came in tremendous gusts from the northwest, with the curious result of keeping the south sidewalks of all the crosstown streets clear of snow (although sheathed in ice), while the north sidewalks and stoops were buried in drifts. The pavements were sheets of ice, so that crossing them in the high wind with nothing to hold on to was a terrifying experience.

A young chambermaid who had left home before dawn to get to her job found herself falling down in the middle of Fifth Avenue. Desperately she caught hold of the only support available, the bridle of a passing horse. A policeman rescued her as she was about to be dragged under the carriage wheels.

"God damn!" he yelled at her, somewhat less chivalrous than New York's Finest were supposed to be, "What be you doin'?"

31

The air was full of strange flying objects: signs torn loose from shops, bits of glass from broken windows, ashes and dust, cardboard boxes, newspapers, umbrellas, hats, awnings, frozen sparrows. New York streets, even in the best of weather, were none too safe or pleasant, and they always presented something of an obstacle course for pedestrians. Grocers kept bins of coal for sale in front of their stores and cluttered up half the sidewalk with tin-roofed storage sheds. Store windows protruded several feet into sidewalk space, as did awnings, with the poles to hold them up. There were also bootblacks' stands and newspaper kiosks, as well as the carts and baskets belonging to assorted peddlers. Refuse was swept or thrown from houses into the gutters, and open barrels of ashes sat on the sidewalks for days, awaiting collection. Because New York City blocks have no back alleys, refuse collections have always been made in front; and in 1888, collections were somewhat haphazard. Littering was not a crime, and even well-bred people thought nothing of disposing of newspapers by simply dropping them for the wind to take hither and yon.

The pavements themselves were often in a state of disarray because of building, wrecking, or digging. The raised rails upon which the horsecars ran prevented wagons from passing each other. Near the ferries and the Brooklyn Bridge, wagon owners were in the habit of leaving their vehicles in the streets overnight, while they took their horses home with them. Worst of all, a heavy rain was apt to cause an overflow of sewage. Where the pavements were made of cobblestones, as they mostly were, sewage and offal of all kinds sank down into the cracks and stayed there until spells of sunny weather dried it into noisome dust.

Monday, March 12, happened to be the day chosen that year by the Police Department (which took care of sanitary matters when it could find time) for a biannual thorough street cleaning. Gangs of laborers were supposed to report that morning to sweep and scrub the streets and collect wagonloads of refuse and filth to be dumped into the rivers.

Street-cleaning techniques in New York at that time were no worse than they were in London, and perhaps better than in Calcutta, but definitely behind Paris and many other major cities. One trouble was that the job of street cleaner was looked down on by all other workers. Laborers were hired by the day at the lowest of wages: $1.20 for ten hours of work. A man could often make as much by sweeping crossings on a free-lance basis and collecting pennies from passersby, or by sending his children out to do the same.

On Monday morning, it soon became apparent that New York's streets were not going to be cleaned that day. Nor was it useful to start shoveling the snow, because the wild wind immediately blew it about again. The wind also caught up the dust and ash, swirled it about with icy snow, and flung the whole concoction into the faces of people and beasts. As some of those who experienced it said later, it was "like a barrage of bullets," "like sand," "like lashes of a whip," and "like flying glass." They recalled how strange it was to see passersby with bloody faces, "as if a battle were going on." Even men who, like Sergeant Francis Long, had been on the Arctic tundra or the western plains, said they had never known anything to match that day on the streets of New York.

The blizzard may have seemed even worse than it was because no one was prepared or dressed for it. Ordinary city clothes wouldn't do. The fine snow penetrated mufflers and gloves, and the wind took any hat that wasn't tied on and blew it over the rooftops. People tried, more or less in vain, to protect their feet and legs with newspapers, extra stockings, straw wine-bottle covers, or strips of carpet.

Those whose jobs took them out before dawn were the least

prepared, for they had no idea what they were getting into. These included milkmen, drivers of butcher's and baker's wagons, mail carriers, workers at the wholesale markets, and employees of the transportation systems.

William Brubacker was a milkman. Every morning he left his home in lower Manhattan at 2:30 A.M., crossed to Jersey City on the ferry with his horse and wagon, met a milk train, and returned to Manhattan by five o'clock to start delivering milk. On Monday, March 12, the trip took him two hours longer than usual, and by the time he had maneuvered his wagon over half his route he was exhausted and had frostbitten ears. He said later that his horse had already turned toward the stable three times. "He had more sense than I."

At about ten o'clock, Brubacker stopped at a saloon for a resuscitative glass of whiskey. The bartender told him he looked to be in terrible shape, and said that if he had remained outdoors another hour he would have frozen to death. "He made me walk the floor for ten minutes and I had another drink. I began to realize myself that I did not stop any too soon." Brubacker then went straight home and stayed there for the next four days. No milk was coming through, anyway. On the fifth day he resumed his usual routine, but the milk he picked up in Jersey City was solid ice.

Brubacker did not mention whether or not his horse recovered, but certainly that Monday was a terrible day for horses. Horsecars, each pulled by two horses, had been the mainstay of New York's transportation system for nearly sixty years, enabling working people to live beyond walking distance from their jobs. The horsecars were always crowded, and life for the horses that pulled them was far from easy. But on that dreadful morning, they kept loosing their footing on the icy pavement. Where deep snow had accumulated on the tracks, they could not get through, even when they were sent out in teams of four or six, with two drivers, and even when the conductors and passengers got out and pushed. The drivers, who rode outside the stove-heated passenger cars, soon became dangerously chilled. The result was that before mid-morning, many more streets had been rendered impassable by horsecars abandoned where they stood. Drivers had turned their passengers out and led the horses back to their stables.

"I do not know when business will be resumed," said a street railway official when queried by a reporter. "Our worst difficulty is the wind. The horses suffer terribly." The companies did have snowplows, which in ordinary snowstorms could keep the tracks clear. But today they simply slid off the tracks. Sixteen horses, accompanied by twenty men shoveling, failed to make any progress.

A sleigh certainly seemed like a better idea than any wheeled vehicle. One resourceful businessman (who did not give his name when interviewed, so let us call him Jones) rented one, with driver, at a livery stable. He was intent on reaching his downtown office from his home on West 128th Street.

"The driver told me the horse was liable to run away if he got excited, but he didn't get excited. He started off at a fast trot. . . . The air was so full of little fine needles of snow and the wind tore by us at such a rate that that horse staggered about like a drunken man. But he was game. He put his head down and trotted ahead in the teeth of the blast. His mane and tail were masses of ice, and his hide was thickly veneered with it. My eyeglasses were covered with ice so thick that I had to lick it off every five minutes."

Heading down Third Avenue, they passed brewers' wagons drawn by as many as ten Normandy horses, "but even their great strength was not enough to pull the wagons through some drifts. The drivers were lashing the poor beasts with their whips and cursing them with great vigor. . . . The sleet striking my face made me feel as if it was raining carpet tacks. My moustache was frozen solid, and my eyebrows, too, and little icicles formed on my eyelashes and got into my eyes. They hurt like hot cinders."

At 84th Street Mr. Jones and his driver stopped and bought toboggan caps. The driver remarked, "I'm an old New York tough. I'm sixty-one, and I've lived here, man and boy, all my life. But I'll be ——— if ever I seen the likes o' this ride, an' I doan wanter."

"And still," continued Mr. Jones, "that good horse went staggering ahead. We tilted nearly over several times and twice we ran into pillars of the elevated road, for we couldn't see where we were going half the time." But they did get to Jones's office. After ascertaining that no business was likely to be transacted, Jones quickly locked up, went to a hotel, and took a room for the night. What happened to the "good horse" and his good driver we do not know.

Animals in America would have suffered even more had it not been for the American Society for the Prevention of Cruelty to Animals and its founder, Henry Bergh. As it happened, Bergh had been lying mortally ill at his Fifth Avenue home during the past week, and just as the blizzard was bearing down on the city, he died. Twenty years earlier, he had almost single-handedly brought about the passage of laws in this country regarding animal care. Having done a tour of duty at the American embassy in St. Petersburg, he became obsessed by the cruelty of Russian peasants toward their animals; and on his way home, he stopped in England to learn about the Royal SPCA and how it had been created. Then, back in New York, he devoted the rest of his life to the fight for animal protection. Because of his efforts, it had become a misdemeanor by act or neglect to maliciously kill, injure, or cruelly beat an animal, whether one's own or not. By 1888, branches of the ASPCA had sprung up all over the nation, and stricter laws had followed the first ones, even though many people regarded such restraints as an outrageous invasion of their civil rights.

Bergh and his colleagues were wont to stop horsecars in the street if they thought the horses were being abused or if the cars were overloaded. Bergh would unharness the horses and lead them back to their stables, leaving stranded cars full of fuming passengers. His methods were high-handed, but they brought results. By 1888, the issue of kindness to animals, which few Americans had given much thought to, had come to seem a normal and proper legal province.

If people demanded hard work of their horses, they were as likely to ask the same of themselves. One of the striking differences between the 1880s and the 1980s is the earlier decade's passionate allegiance to the work ethic. In our time, most working persons who found their front doors completely blocked by snow would be more than likely to stay inside. But in 1888 great numbers of workers, from the president of the New York Central Railroad down to fourteen-year-old Western Union messenger boys did not even see this as a choice. Getting to work was what they *had* to do. That compulsion drove them on that blizzard morning to such extremes as to get out of their homes by sliding down snow-buried steps on an ironing board, or to leap from a window into a snowdrift, or to walk a hundred icy blocks worrying all the time about being late. One good reason, of course, was that workers knew how merciless the boss or the foreman could be. It was usual practice for employees to be fined for lateness and fired for absence, no matter what the excuse. Jobs were not easy to find and, without references, almost impossible. Unemployment insurance was still half a century away.

Children, too, were early imbued with this lemming drive, and during the blizzard there were instances of their insisting on going to school even when their parents urged them not to—which suggests that Victorian parents were not always as authoritarian, or children as obedient, as myth would have us believe. In Brooklyn, ten-year-old Rufus Billings, on Nostrand Avenue, defied his parents and announced that he was going to school. When they hid his boots, Rufus found them and rushed out into the storm. At the school door he found about a dozen like-minded children—but no teachers or janitor—and they stood there for more than an hour, lashed by snow and wind, until the principal arrived and formally dismissed them.

Another dutiful child was ten-year-old Sam Strong, who lived in Harlem (then a middle-class white neighborhood) with his uncle and aunt, Mr. and Mrs. Charles Green, a childless couple who prided themselves on their well-regulated household, on dressing well, and on responding to their duty in bringing up an orphaned nephew.

On Monday morning, March 12, Mrs. Green was expecting her dressmaker, who would be spending the entire week at the Green house, making Mrs. Green's spring wardrobe. Since the dressmaker was paid by the hour, Mrs. Green rose early and went to the sewing room to make sure that all necessary supplies were on hand. After making a list of what was lacking— whalebones and dressmaker's chalk, and a large, strong needle for sewing corsets—she dispatched her nephew to fetch these articles from the notions store before he went to school. Perhaps she did not even glance out of the window, the weather being of no interest to one who intends to remain at home all week. Sam, however, had seen from the window a man go sprawling on the icy sidewalk opposite their house, and had noted that the areaway gate had disappeared in snow. He mentioned these matters to his aunt, who merely bade him put on his high rubber boots (a recent invention, soft rubber with a strap to hold them on above the knee), plus a heavy overcoat, and a woolen cap, gloves, and muffler.

"There, you could go to the North Pole in that outfit," Mrs. Green said. "Hurry now, so you won't be late for school."

Sam could not find the front steps and went down the stoop more sliding than walking. Despite the bitter wind and blinding snow, he liked the adventurous flavor of it all, and he plunged off through waist-deep drifts. He went east to Lenox Avenue and then turned north, bound for Brady's notion store on 125th Street. On Lenox Avenue, he came face to face with the wind, which unceremoniously picked him up off his feet and deposited him in a drift much higher than his head. There he remained for ten or fifteen minutes, depleting his strength by useless efforts to extract himself. At last, when he had begun to feel much more frightened than adventurous, a policeman came along and pulled him from the drift. "You hadn't ought to be out in this, Sonny," he chided. "You go straight home."

But Sam struggled on, apparently driven by the same blind obedience as the boy in "Casabianca," that favorite poem of Victorians in which "the boy stood on the burning deck / Whence all but him had fled." (The reason the boy stood there was that his father had told him to wait for him. But the father drowned, and the boy went down with the ship.)

Sam passed abandoned wagons and carriages. On 125th Street, a cable car struggled weakly along. This line kept up service that morning longer than any horse-drawn vehicle, but was finally defeated by ice in the cogs.

The few people Sam met staggered by with their hands

over their ears or clutching their hats. Forty-one years later, when Sam—now **Dr.** Strong—became head of the Society of Blizzard Men and Blizzard Ladies, he said it was the wind, more than anything, that stood out in his mind when he thought back to the blizzard.

"When I could get down out of the cutting wind behind a snowdrift, I was all right, but traveling took every ounce of power in my body." Sometimes other pedestrians would assist him through the hardest places.

When he reached the spot where he knew Brady's should be, he could hardly find it. Its door and show window were buried in drifts, and there was clearly no possibility of buying anything there that day. He pushed on for about another half-mile, finding no stores open, notions or otherwise. When he stopped a pedestrian to ask if he knew where a corset needle could be bought, he "learned a few new and attractive profane expressions to add to my already fair vocabulary of cuss words, and with his help I about-faced and started the homeward trek."

Going home was even more difficult, as the drifts seemed to grow more formidable every minute. He became stuck half a dozen times and might well have died, had it not been for the friendly hands of strangers who came to his rescue. He did not reach his home until nearly noon, having been gone four hours. He clawed and fought his way up the buried stoop and was pulled into the house by his aunt and uncle. Now thoroughly alarmed, they had been watching for him all morning. Uncle had not gone to work, nor had the dressmaker come. So much snow tumbled into the vestibule with Sam that it had to be shoveled out before the double doors could be closed.

His aunt said nothing harsh to him, but he was nevertheless disconsolate.

"Although I had fought the snow for more than four hours, I had failed in my mission. There were many tears. A rub with alcohol after I was in bed with glass bottles filled with hot water, a big slug of raw whiskey and some food, and I was asleep, not waking until night and then only for more food and drink. I was exhausted."

2

Getting There

FIFTY THOUSAND NEW YORKERS depended on the els to take them to their jobs and back. There were four lines running north and south—on Second, Third, Sixth, and Ninth avenues—plus connecting tracks on a few crosstown streets. Although it was now possible for people employed in lower Manhattan to live in the upper part of the island and even as far away as the Bronx, there were never enough trains at rush hour—let alone seats—to accommodate them all. It had become clear to forward-looking persons, such as Mayor Hewitt and many newspaper editors, that the city was in desperate need of an underground railroad; but so far the state legislature in Albany, which controlled the necessary funds, had been unable to address such a bold and unprecedented idea. The municipal Board of Aldermen might have got the ball rolling; but unfortunately this body was in disarray, twenty out of twenty-two aldermen having recently been indicted for sharing a $500,000 bribe.

The dirty, noisy, ugly els were a public nuisance as well as a public salvation. Their two-story-high iron trestles, disfiguring what might have been beautiful avenues, supported two-way, narrow-gauge tracks, over which ran scaled-down steam locomotives and wooden passenger cars. The smokestacks of the little engines spewed soot on pedestrians below. In wet weather, greasy black drops dripped from the trestles. Sparks sometimes started fires, and the sudden rumbling of a train could bring about street accidents, as horses bolted and wagons overturned. A popular song of the 1880s was entitled "The Rapid Transit Galop" and called for fast-and-furious dancing. Streetwise horses soon learned to be calmer than the dancers.

At first, the public was fearful that any small mishap might cause the trains to tip over and plummet into the street below. For a better center of gravity, cars were made with "drop-belly" sides. But, in the sixty-odd years of operation and millions of miles of travel, a total of thirty-one people died in accidents. Only one passenger car (empty) and four locomotives ever toppled into the street.

In 1888, how to substitute electric power for steam without electrocuting the passengers was not quite understood, but it would be in a dozen years. The problem of what to do with fifty thousand passengers in case of a blizzard had not come up until Monday morning, March 12, 1888. Now, suddenly, the problem was urgent.

The main difficulties were that the blinding snow reduced visibility to a few yards; the tracks were sheathed in ice; the switches froze and had to be constantly defrosted by men with pails of saltwater and brooms; and, because the telegraph wires were down, the general dispatchers could not get in touch with the station dispatchers, creating a dangerous chaos. By rush hour that morning two locomotives were needed to pull even shortened trains, and they had to advance very cautiously.

Delays grew longer and longer. Station platforms, high and open to the storm, became jammed with miserable commuters and many trains went right by them without stopping.

At about 7 A.M. on Monday, March 12, a salesman of haberdashery, E. E. Handel, boarded the Third Avenue line at 84th Street. After leaving the station, the train exceeded the legal limit of twelve miles per hour. "We went so fast out of the regular it became alarming," Handel told friends later. "I said we will have a collision and sure enough it came."

Between 76th Street and the next station, 67th Street, was a steep grade. In icy weather, engineers were likely to skip the 76th Street stop in order to get up steam to carry the train uphill. Twenty minutes before the collision, a train had stopped at 76th, pulling up just beyond the station so as to limit the number of boarding passengers to those who could scramble onto the rear platform. Then the train stood still for twenty minutes, because the engineer could barely perceive other trains ahead and dared not try the grade until the way was clear.

The train carrying Mr. Handel had two engines. The engineer of the first one, Samuel Towle, had been informed at 84th Street that no downtown train had passed for twenty minutes, and he therefore determined to lay on steam and get to 67th Street. According to a newspaper report, "He therefore put on all steam down the grade and approached the 76th Street station at a speed much greater than that usually attained by elevated trains."

In the blinding snow, Towle did not see the standing train until he was less than a block away from it. When the engineer and fireman of the second engine on Towle's train saw it looming up, they promptly deserted their posts and jumped to the trestle, surviving without serious injury. Towle and his fireman stayed put, undoubtedly preventing a major disaster. Despite braking, Towle's locomotive plowed into the rear of the train ahead with enough force to cause both Towle's engine and the rear car ahead to rise into the air and come down again partly off the tracks and leaning against the station. Fortunately, most of the passengers standing on the rear platform of the struck train had had time to jump back to the station platform. Others, with all the strength of terror, had forced their way forward into the packed rear car. In this melee, about a dozen people were injured severely enough to be taken to hospitals. Those uninjured, though badly shaken, were able to leave the trains in a fairly orderly manner, edging their way along the trestle to be boosted up to the station platform by kind bystanders.

Meanwhile, the unmanned and unbraked second engine of Towle's train had rammed into his tender, pinning him between it and the boiler. His loyal fireman, who had suffered only a shaking up, got onto the platform and organized others to attempt to free Towle, whose cries of pain were terrible to hear.

The passengers in Towle's train behaved badly. Someone cried "Fire!" although there was none. Panic ensued and men began to break windows. The New York *Sun* reported later that they "thrust the screaming women aside" to crawl out of the cars. Mr. Handel said, "I shouted to take it easy—but that was useless. . . . the people were wild."

Mr. Handel heeded his own advice and took it easy, waiting until he could walk out of the train. Then, instead of going home, as many now felt justified in doing, he continued his journey on foot, because "I felt I could not afford to lose my position as salesman." The haberdashery where he worked was at 10th Street and Broadway, and the three-and-a-half-mile walk took him four hours.

At the 76th Street station, police and firemen arrived after a considerable delay and used axes to free poor Towle, but he died as he was being lifted to the platform.

The Third Avenue line was in a chaotic state for the rest of the day, but its counterpart on Second Avenue managed to keep going, after a fashion. William Dewey, a fireman on that line, was proud of helping to get his train from the uptown yard (leaving at 6:45 A.M.) as far as 19th Street (arriving an hour late, at 8:20), where it became stuck and stayed put for five hours—fortunately, at a station, so that passengers were free to get off. The only food Dewey ate all day came from friendly souls whose windows overlooked the el tracks. They made coffee and corned beef sandwiches and passed them to him across a four-foot abyss by means of a clinker hook.

The train at last moved on downtown, and then back uptown, completing one round trip that day. On the northbound trip, the cars were so crowded that stations had to be skipped, "leaving a howling mob of disappointed ticket-buying patrons." By and large, the crowds were good-natured but when trains did stop there was rough pushing and shoving, and many would-be riders narrowly escaped from falling off the trestle.

Without the telegraph, no one at the headquarters of the four elevated lines knew what was going on, and it was afternoon before they even heard of the 76th Street accident. The manager never got to headquarters at all that day, and the superintendent came in and went right out again, to deal with the monumental confusion on the Sixth Avenue line.

Mollie Katz, a maiden lady in her thirties who lived on West 27th Street, boarded a Sixth Avenue el at about 7:30 A.M. She was on her way to take the ferry to Jersey City, where she worked as a clerk. The train was very crowded and she had to stand. (On ordinary days, gentlemen often gave her a seat, but today the atmosphere was so fraught with anxiety that gentlemen had become scarce.) Advancing by fits and starts, the train

46

reached a point near 3rd Street where the tracks entered a long curve, and there it came to a dead halt. Five . . . ten . . . thirty minutes went by . . . then an hour. The train shivered and rocked in the wind, and the engineer had turned off the steam, so there was no heat other than that generated by the tightly packed bodies. Baths were not an everyday affair in the 1880s, and dry cleaning was expensive. The atmosphere would have become fetid except that from time to time "desperate men . . . looking for ladders or some other way of getting out of their trap" would drag open one of the doors, whereupon "the storm would rush in with a scream, dashing its burden of snow into people's faces almost half the length of the car." Two hours went by. Then three.

The New York *Sun* was fortunate in having an eyewitness reporter on board, who next day wrote a full account of his experiences. "The mathematical fiend, who seems to infest every place, came near creating some alarm . . . He figured that there were not less than eighty trains on the downtown track, consisting of five cars each, with an average of 100 passengers in each car, who—as they were nearly all men—might be averaged at 150 pounds weight each. That would give a total of 3,000 tons of human beings, in addition to the enormous weight of the rolling stock, and engines and snow, all on one side of the structure, and, he said, 'it would be nothing strange if the whole business slumped over sidewise into the street.' But as people observed that it didn't slump they appeared to become accustomed to the situation and resigned to take their chances. Then he went to figuring on how many would be likely to get deadly pneumonia from the savage draughts of air."

By now it was lunchtime. Those who had brought box lunches ate them and some shared tidbits with their neighbors.

" 'If we could only smoke, this situation would be a little more tolerable,' suggested somebody.

" 'Happy thought!' suggested somebody else, 'for the company's rules prescribe that anybody who smokes shall be put off the train, and that being what we all want, we should all smoke.'

"There were five ladies in the car. The first one, asked if she would object to smoking, said very pleasantly: 'Not at all; I would be happy to see you gentlemen find some mitigation of our common discomfort.'

"The second said, 'No; I wish I could smoke with you.'

"The third replied: 'Certainly. I am not so selfish as to deny to others a pleasure that I cannot share.'

"The fourth also gave pleasant and ready consent."

There was a fifth woman at the far end of the car, but the would-be smokers decided that "she was too hard to get at to be asked, and she looked as if she could stand smoke, or pretty much anything else, so the ventilators above were opened, and a few cigars and cigarettes were lighted.

"Instantly a little ferret-faced fellow with a red nose, who announced himself as being in company with the fifth woman, made a tumultuous kick. He declared that the smoke made her very sick, that she was almost fainting, and he seemed upon the verge of apoplexy. The cigars and cigarettes were extinguished in deference to the woman, and a gloom settled down over the previously jolly party."

Some of the braver and sturdier men climbed down to the track and crawled on hands and knees along the windy trestle back to the station. No one could see out of the windows, because they were completely iced over, but somehow the news spread that men in the street had brought a ladder, placed it against the trestle, and were charging fifteen cents to anyone wishing to use it.

Miss Katz got out of the train and watched while several men made the descent. "With so much snow and ice," she said later, "it was some stunt to . . . balance oneself on a tie or rail, then reach for the ladder ends, swing around and descend." She dared not try it, but two black men later lashed two ladders together, so that the top rungs of one were even with the trestle. Driven, no doubt, by extreme discomfort, Miss Katz got up the courage to try, and made it, to the sound of huzzahs from below. She learned afterward that nearly all the other women and the fainter-hearted men had waited in the train until nearly dusk, when extra locomotives finally arrived to pull the cars back to the nearest station.

Miss Katz "lost no time repairing to a tiny coffee and sinker [doughnut] place near 9th Street." She had had nothing to eat that day, as she usually breakfasted near the ferry terminal, at Smith and McNeil's Hotel, which had a popular restaurant where one could get steak, potatoes, bread, butter, and coffee, all for twenty cents. Aborting her trip to New Jersey, the resourceful Miss Katz reached a friend's house on 12th Street, where she remained for the rest of the blizzard.

One of her fellow passengers, a bookkeeper named John Porter, not only executed the hazardous ladder maneuver, but did it carrying a young woman—a total stranger—over his shoulder. Halfway down the ladder he missed his footing, but luckily he and his burden fell without harm into a deep snowbank.

Women needed help in this blizzard, for few of them were as robust as men, and their clothing put them at a distinct disadvantage. In their voluminous skirts and high heeled boots or shoes they easily lost their balance and were flattened by the wind like paper dolls. Their large hats, festooned with birds, wax fruit, posies, and giant bows, went sailing down the street. Veils, which were supposed to help keep hats on heads, became tattered or so caked with ice as to cut off all vision. Dyes began to run, causing the unhappy faces behind the veils to turn a streaky blue or mottled green. A reporter for the New York *Times* admired "the handy way in which women managed their clothes and fought their way through snowbanks. . . . Tied up in veils and mufflers they pluckily fought against wind and snow." But he added that he had seen at least twenty girls fall within five blocks.

Men were better off, but their bowler hats and derbies blew away, and leather shoes were quickly soaked through. A men's furnishings store in the Wall Street area did a brisk business, even though its awning had collapsed and customers had to climb over it in order to get inside. The store had already put away its woolen gloves for the summer, but quickly got them out again and sold all forty-five dozen pairs within a few hours. A resourceful clerk invented a new kind of wool pull-on cap by cutting jersey bathing trunks through the center and tying each leg with a piece of string. These quickly sold out, as did ten dozen pairs of earmuffs. There was also a run on rubber thigh-boots meant for fishing.

Stockbrokers who had had to walk to work that morning stopped to buy fresh collars and shirts (a sociological note that the *Sun* reported, finding it "peculiar and interesting"). But when they arrived at the Stock Exchange they found the floor nearly deserted. Instead of the usual five hundred brokers, there were only twenty-one; and the private wires to Chicago, Boston, and elsewhere were all dead. "Brother Jones" (Edward D. Jones, of Dow, Jones), was among the absent. He had started downtown on the el from his home in Harlem, but after taking four hours to get as far as 23rd Street, he and a contingent of other brokers had called it a day. They booked rooms in one of the good hotels and then sat down to a long, bibulous lunch. Other Wall Street men, more dedicated (or perhaps more susceptible to losing their jobs), walked when the els gave out. Some paid as much as forty dollars for cabs that usually charged fifty cents for the first mile and twenty-five cents for each additional half-mile; and two came half the way in a butcher cart, until the butcher boy and his horse decided to head for the stable. By noon, about a hundred brokers were at the exchange, along with twenty customers. One wire was working to Chicago, and 15,200 shares had been traded. The chairman, deciding that was no way to run a stock exchange, banged his ivory hammer and announced that all dealings would be suspended and deliveries held over until the next day. It was the first time in history that the Stock Exchange had closed on account of weather.

Other exchanges such as the Cotton, the Maritime, and the Coffee exchanges also closed early, and the Real Estate Exchange never opened at all. Business was light at the Custom House, where two-thirds of the employees were absent. Most of the female inspectors showed up, however, probably because their jobs were more vulnerable, employment of female customs inspectors being still only a cautious experiment.

At the city's courts, there was very little action that day. In the court of Common Pleas the deputy clerk arrived and waited, with one other clerk, until 1 P.M., when the judge arrived in a milk sleigh. After formally opening and adjourning the court for the day, His Honor took the two clerks over to the Astor House for lunch and a few nips. At City Hall, one couple presented themselves to be married, and were fortunate in finding a judge on hand. The bridegroom being Dutch and the bride Russian, neither appeared fazed by snow and ice.

One might suppose that prosperous men would have been able to take a day off, but in many cases it was the boss who turned up first at the shop or office door. Not only did he have important business to transact (bonds fell due, rents had to be paid, mortgages collected, deals consummated) but, like humbler folk, he, too, felt driven. He had to get there in order to unlock the door for his employees, or to set them a good example, or simply because he was (as we would say now) programmed to get there. Getting there was one reason for his success—and well he knew it.

In mid-morning, Theodore Roosevelt, who was living at 689 Madison Avenue, at 62nd Street, had an appointment down at Second Avenue and 11th Street with the secretary of the New-York Historical Society. Although it was an appointment of no great importance, T.R. was not a man to neglect commitments. Walking three miles, he arrived at the society's offices to find no one there but a couple of clerks. The secretary, Charles Isham, he was told, had not been heard from that day, nor was he expected, since he lived on 61st Street (around the corner from the Roosevelts).

The future president walked back uptown, kept warm, no doubt, by his high dudgeon. He sent a note to Mr. Isham as soon as he arrived home: "I went down to the Society Rooms to see you today but I presume the blizzard kept you at home."

At the Murray Hill Hotel, Samuel Clemens—Mark Twain— looked out of his bedroom window and decided to stay there until it stopped snowing. He had come to New York from his home in Hartford on Saturday in order to attend a stag dinner given by his friend Charles A. Dana, publisher of the *Sun,* in honor of the English actor Henry Irving, who, with Ellen Terry, was in the last week of a winter-long engagement in *Faust.* Clemens' wife, Olivia, was to have arrived on Monday, and he hoped she was not at that moment on a train halfway to New York. He had tried to get through to her by telegraph, but with no luck. In fact, Livy had made the decision on her own to stay at home. Meanwhile, Clemens sat gloomily at the Murray Hill, writing her a letter:

GETTING THERE

Blast that blasted dinner party at Dana's! But for that, I—ah! Well, I'm tired, tired calling myself names. Why, I could have been at home all this time. Whereas, here I have been Crusoing on a desert hotel—out of wife, out of children, out of line, and out of cigars, out of every blamed thing in the world that I've any use for. Great Scott!*

In 1888, there were still more private houses in New York City than multiple dwellings, although many older houses, built for single families, were now used as boardinghouses or as shops with living quarters above. The poor lived in tenements; the rich and prosperous, in commodious if stuffy four-story brownstones. A prototype of the apartment house was the Dakota, completed in 1884 and so called because it stood all alone in the wilds of the West Side (at Central Park West and 72nd Street, where it still flourishes). Its success at attracting middle- and upper-class residents prompted the construction of similar buildings. Each apartment often provided more floor space than a house and required fewer servants. Apartment hotels were popular with bachelors and young married couples because they offered light cooking facilities and also a restaurant downstairs that served meals or sent them up. Despite prejudice against multiple dwellings because tenements had such a bad name, the well-to-do began to see their advantages. To call such quarters French flats helped their acceptance; after all, the very best sort of Parisians had been living like that for years.

One New York couple who had taken to apartment living were Mr. and Mrs. George D. Baremore. After several years at

*Contrary to popular belief, Mark Twain did not say, "Everybody complains about the weather, but nobody ever does anything about it." That statement came from his friend, the author and editor Charles Dudley Warner, and was first published in 1890, in the Hartford *Courant*.

53

the Dakota, the Baremores, with their two children, had recently moved to the imposing new Osborne, at 205 West 57th Street. When it opened in 1885, it was the tallest building in the city: eleven stories. The Osborne offered all the amenities of the Dakota (restaurant, ballroom, separate suites of guest rooms) plus shops and a doctor's office. Each apartment boasted electric lights, steam heat, ash or mahogany woodwork, and decorative windows of Tiffany stained glass. Literally topping off all this splendor was a croquet lawn on the roof.

Monday, March 12, was not a day for croquet.

"Oh, George!" cried Mrs. Baremore, looking out of the high windows at breakfast time. "You'd better stay at home today. It's snowing so hard I can't even see the street."

Mr. Baremore reminded her jocularly that people who live in the sky can't always expect to be able to see the street. He was a successful dealer in imported hops, thirty-seven years old, and the head of his own company with offices at the Battery. He had to get to work.

The Osborne stood alone in its block, surrounded by vacant lots and receiving the full brunt of the wicked northwest wind. When Baremore left the lobby (a wonderland of marble, mahogany, mosaic, and frescoes) the doorman could hardly open the door for him.

"Cab, sir?"

Baremore said the el would be much quicker, and set off. To ambitious New Yorkers, time was of more importance than luxury. The idea was to earn luxury and live surrounded by it later.

To reach the nearest Sixth Avenue el station, Baremore had to walk four blocks. The wind on 56th Street was bad enough, but when he turned down Sixth Avenue, it was on him like a wild animal and hurled him into a snowdrift. Unaccustomed as he was to being pushed around, Baremore was probably more outraged than anything else. By hanging on to a lamppost, he got to his feet again and pressed forward. There were a few others going his way, but he hardly noticed them. He was too busy keeping his footing, holding his muffler over his mouth to keep out the flying snow, and grasping the brim of his new English bowler with his free hand. It took him half an hour to reach the el station and nearly ten minutes to ascend the long slippery flight of stairs to the platform.

With a crowd of fellow sufferers, he waited an hour until the stationmaster announced that there would be no more trains on that line in the foreseeable future, but that he had heard the Ninth Avenue el was moving. The assemblage—mostly men, with a scattering of women—looked at each other, smiled grimly, and dispersed. George Baremore was determined not to be defeated by this setback. It was his businessman's habit to view any problem as a challenge, and then to attack it as if it were a dragon and he Saint George on a charger. So far, this attitude had been important to Baremore's success.

He decided to walk along 53rd Street beneath the el tracks. The snow was not so deep there, nor the wind so fierce. The street might have been that of a pillaged city. Deserted wagons and trucks stood where drivers had abandoned them. He passed a horse so deeply stuck in a snowdrift that only its head and neck were visible. It was dead and frozen stiff. Suddenly he became aware of something plopping onto his hat from time to time, and discovered that the bodies of frozen sparrows were dropping from the nooks and crannies of the el girders.

Baremore had reached Seventh Avenue and was attempting to cross it when a tremendous gust of wind came down upon him. This part of Seventh Avenue is on rising ground, and the wind, having gathered momentum in the empty reaches of Central Park, was sweeping madly along it at close to fifty miles an hour. It picked up Baremore, banged his head on a stanchion of the el trestle, and threw him into a drift twice his height. It took his hat and even blew his coat open across the chest, so that when, half-stunned, he looked down, he saw his gold watch and chain glinting there. Perhaps the thought crossed his mind of giving a cabdriver the gold watch and chain to take him downtown; that might be the way to meet this challenge. And he put his hand on the watch and grasped it.

But George Baremore never got downtown. Before dawn the next morning a policeman struggling up Seventh Avenue on his regular beat noticed a hand sticking out of a snowdrift. He kicked the snow away and discovered the frozen body of a well-dressed man. The other hand clutched a gold watch and chain, and in his pocket were two or three recent letters addressed to George D. Baremore, The Osborne Flats.

3

Trying Circumstances

FROM THE DAILY RECORDS of the New York Weather Bureau, Monday, March 12, 1888:

The assistants on duty at this office are deserving of the greatest praise for their promptness and most willing effort under such trying circumstances to keep the instruments in proper working order and all the routine duties both in and out of the office, reflects credit upon their courage. . . . not a man was absent at that office and all reached here at the peril of their lives.

Sergeant Francis Long, as usual, got to work on time. His walk over the Brooklyn Bridge took him longer than usual, but he had allowed for that and had found it interesting: so much snow that the water below was invisible, and so much ice that fellow pedestrians kept falling down and a woman had to be carried from the bridge unconscious. The footwalk was closed soon after Long got across it.

He was first at the office, but very soon his chief, Elias ("Farmer") Dunn, arrived, and so did all the others. Since they were military men, perhaps their sense of duty was especially strong. One man, whose suburban train had stalled above 145th Street, had walked and crawled for more than a mile on top of stalled trains.

The whole staff was soon in a turmoil. It was discovered that the anemometer, which measured wind velocity, had frozen stiff. Without it, vital records of the storm would be lost. The instrument, located on the tower of the Equitable Assurance Building, was attached to a sliding iron pipe in two sections, held by a thumbscrew to the top of a pole. The pole was four inches in diameter and rose twenty-five feet above the tower, which in turn soared 172 feet above the street. The only way to fix the anemometer was to climb the pole.

As Chief Dunn wrote many years later, the wind was gusting "about 75 miles an hour in a driving spicular [sic] of snow and ice," and "there was no one I could get for love or money to climb that pole under such conditions." It seemed that duty had its limits, even in the army, and Dunn was unwilling to make the request an order.

Then Sergeant Long came to him and said, "Mr. Dunn, if you will let me I will fix it."

"Long," said Dunn, "you are too heavy a man. The pole will snap and I will be responsible for a dead man."

"Sir," said Long, "it will be at my own risk."

For Long, there appeared to be no question: this was something he had to do. Possibly he felt the need to prove himself one more time, but we will never know, because he was not the sort of man to discuss or analyze his feelings. Could he have doubted his own courage? During ten years with the Army of the West, he had certainly fought Indians, but had escaped the awful fate of Custer's troops. In the Arctic, he had been the crack shot and the

58

hunter, bringing in a four-hundred-pound bear just when the party had resorted to eating their leather belts. But, later, hunting seals, his Eskimo guide had drowned while trying to maneuver the animals into range of Long's gun. Did Long feel responsible? And just before the six survivors were rescued, General Greely had named Long one of three men who were to draw lots for the task of shooting an enlisted man who had been stealing food. Was Long the executioner? And had he, as hunter and cook, somehow gotten more to eat than those who died? A man with those experiences might need to undertake a new challenge, one in which his courage could not be questioned.

Chief Dunn wrote:

He climbed that slim pole without any support, adjusted the instrument and replaced some wiring with one hand while several assistants and myself tried to support the pole. The wind pressure was so great that it was most difficult for one to stand up, even by holding on, and impossible to get one's breath if facing the wind. Long was nearly frozen, but still he kept on until the instrument was in proper working order. It was a most heroic act and I commended him very highly to our Washington Department. The principal record of that storm would have been lost had it not been for Francis Long.

He was the hunter in the Greely party and those that survived owed their lives to his bravery. When that party was found by Admiral Schley he was the only man that could move and he was found some miles from the camp crawling on his hands and knees half frozen with his gun in his hand, seeking food for his comrades and superior officer, General A. W. Greely.

After Monday, March 12, 1888, little more is recorded about Long's life. A few years later, General Greely received a letter from someone in New York, suggesting that the general speak to Long about his "dissolute habits." Whether Greely did so is not known, nor is the nature of Long's dissolute habits. Long continued to work for the Weather Bureau and eventually became chief forecaster. He suffered a fatal stroke at his desk in 1916, having sat there daily for thirty-two years.

Meanwhile, out at sea, the nine pilot boats that had sailed on Saturday afternoon had encountered the storm. Aboard the *Caldwell F. Colt*, the *World* reporter, William O. Inglis, had been busy making notes, despite his quivering diaphragm. After leaving the Narrows, the *Colt* had headed southward, hoping to contact New York–bound vessels somewhere along the New Jersey coast between Atlantic Highlands and Cape May. On Saturday evening, they passed a big white schooner yacht, *Iroquois*, out of Boston, bound for Florida. Then they spoke the schooner *Sunlight*, but she was bound for New Haven and declined a pilot; and a big black sugar freighter had just taken one aboard.

"The evening was clear and had every promise of fair weather. The sea kept taking liberties with our boat, though, and I lost interest in the marine landscape," wrote Inglis. Again he retired to his berth. Sunday morning was also fair, with no sign of even a distant storm.

During Sunday they sighted the handsomest of the New York pilot schooners, the *William H. Starbuck*, which next morning, at sea in the blinding storm, was to collide with a British freighter and sink with a loss of five lives. The *Colt* was also the last to speak number 18 pilotboat, *Enchantress*, before she vanished forever.

Inglis remained in his bunk through Sunday, although the pilots assured him that what seemed to him rough weather was only a wave or two whipped up by a brisk southeast breeze. Then, at three o'clock on Monday morning, somewhere off New Jersey, "the wind began to back around from the southeast, and presently it began to blow in puffs from the north."

Within an hour, all canvas was reefed, snow was falling, and a northeast gale was in full progress.

"Sick and stupid as I was I could feel the lively boat jumping and plunging like a yearling pony. . . . Pilots sleep soundly, as a rule, through such trifles," but with the barometer needle swerving wildly between 29.60 and 29.80, even the pilots admitted to some concern.

Day came but "was only a little less dark than midnight." About 11:30 A.M., with only the watch on deck, Inglis was dozing "when a big sea hit the poor schooner solidly under the weather bow and lifted her upward and backward as a hard punch in the jaw will lift a man. She was under main storm trysail only, and had been making a good deal of leeway. That is why the wave caught her so heavily. A second great wave hit her in the side as she still hung in the air, and over she went on her beam ends. Everything movable in her banged down from the windward side. Down lay the poor schooner like a horse shot in battle. Her topmasts were under water, and the yawl [the lifeboat], lashed on deck on the starboard side of the mainmast, was lost from sight.

"The sea began to pour in at the main hatch and rushed aft in a green torrent. Also it came surging down the after companion way and burst open the cabin door. The twin floods met and frothed as they chafed at each other. There had been a brisk hard-coal fire in the cabin stove, and that sent up a cloud of steam and gas when the water struck it so that it was impossible to see in the cabin. The shock sent Jim Sayles flying from his berth on the windward side. . . . he landed head first on the ribs of Julius Adler who had rolled out of his berth and lay sprawled on the floor. . . . He scrambled to his feet and started for the deck. He fought his way through the deadly green torrent, hoisted himself by sheer strength through the companionway, and so climbed to the deck that pointed toward heaven instead of lying flat under foot. He tried to ease her off by letting go the foresheet, but there was no sail set forward and that was out of the question.

"I hung meantime, pendulum fashion, out of my berth to windward, or rather skyward, my elbows on either side keeping me from tumbling down and my legs waving to and fro helplessly. It was a bad fix, and I was so frightened, that my teeth would have chattered only there wasn't even time for chattering. About all I can remember is hanging there like a man doing a trick on the parallel bars, and feeling sorry for a dog I once drowned in a bag."

Then, as if by a miracle, the schooner picked herself up. "She rose like a human being, fighting with the awful waves and righted herself as nimbly as a boxer jumps away from a blow. The whole crew were on deck by this time, including [one] who had hurt his back the day before, but forgot his sprain in trying to save his life. They began to work the pumps fore and aft and lightened her all they could. Jim Sayles and Mr. Fairgreaves stayed on deck and managed things, and Julius and George Waldie came below and hauled all the stuff to windward that they could lift. Mr. Waldie picked up six *Heralds* that he had intended to take aboard an incoming ship, but were now soaking, . . . 'The ——— things are too heavy and they'll help to hold her down if she trips again.'

"No man could witness the actions of the pilots and sailors and not feel braced up by their cool pluck. They admitted afterwards that they thought their last moment had come, but they set about saving their ship as coolly as if they were merely maneuvering her in a race. If a poet had been there, and not sea-sick, he could have found lots of inspiration in the way Jim Sayles bolted for that upper deck, after being shot across the cabin head first. His wits never left him. . . . I would like to say a word here, too, about Manuel Gomez, our steward. He had just finished cooking dinner when the schooner, falling down, sent everything flying from the stove. With almost certain death at his heels, that man calmly stood in the galley and fished around for his flying and floating pots and saucepans. He swore at the wave that knocked the schooner down and called it bad names in good Portuguese swear-words. He didn't seem to mind being drowned half so much as he regretted the loss of good soup. Then, seeing me hanging disconsolate by the elbows in the cabin, with woe written all over my sea-sick face, he came in and tried to cheer me up by calling the wave more choice names, and saying it would be all right directly.

"Well, the schooner righted and the hurricane kept trying hard to bowl her over again. Outside it was dark as early dawn, and in the cabin the single swinging lamp showed destruction written everywhere. All the berths to leeward were flooded. The fair white and gold ceiling was blackened and dented where flying hot coals and cinders had struck it. The carpets and rugs were all washing around, and what had been as pretty a cabin as any yachtsman could ask was all a wreck.

"The hurricane was still howling, and the vast waves thumped and shook our boat again and again as they tried to throw her. Four times in ten minutes it seemed to me she was on her beam ends once more, but she righted herself each time without quite getting down. After much trying the crew succeeded in setting a reefed storm trysail on the foremast. That held her a bit closer to the wind, but even then she threatened to fall down again quite often.

"I had often heard about vessels being on their beam ends but I had never comprehended it. It means death. . . . I asked Jim Sayles if he would bet even money that we would see New York again. He said, 'I hope so,' rather confidently. My small hope needed more bracing. Said I to Julius, 'Will you bet 5 to 8 that we come out of this all right?' Said he, 'My lad, we must put our trust in Providence, even if we do come ashore at Newport once in awhile. . . .'

"I had never before had a great deal of experience at being frightened, but I had a surfeit of it for about thirty-six hours."

4

Commuters

A S THE STORM WORSENED, New Yorkers were relieved to note that the Great Bridge continued to stand
without even trembling. Nevertheless, the authorities
thought it prudent to close it to all traffic. They bore in mind
that some ten years before, in Dundee, Scotland, a new and
much admired railway bridge had collapsed in a winter storm,
carrying a passenger train and seventy-five hapless souls into
the River Tay.

One might suppose that in blizzard conditions the ferries
would have seemed more hazardous than the bridge. But the
bridge was newfangled and therefore not quite trustworthy,
while the old side-wheel ferries had been plying the two rivers
and the bay since early in the century and inspired confidence
because they were so familiar. They kept going, or trying to, all
day long, and most of them completed their trips without
incident, even though there were whitecaps on the Hudson,
and, as one awestruck voyager noted, "the river rose like
an ocean."

In the New York City and Brooklyn areas, there were thirty-five ferry lines, eighteen of them plying to and from Manhattan. In the rush hours, they came and went at intervals of five minutes. In good weather there was no more efficient or pleasant means of transportation, and the thousands of working people who journeyed between Manhattan and New Jersey, Staten Island, or Long Island enjoyed an easy commute. But such was not the case on Monday, March 12. A number of ferries were unable to make headway and had to return to their slips. At least one was carried down to the bay and spent several frightening hours adrift there, at one point tipping so far over that water came through the scuppers into the cabin, thoroughly dousing and terrifying the passengers. Another, fully loaded, collided in the Hudson River with a schooner, and as a result a woman was swept from the ladies' cabin and drowned.

Passengers crossing from Staten Island in mid-morning were suddenly appalled to see a schooner bucketing her way across the ferry's path. She was the *Mary Heitman*, dragging her two anchors. Aboard were five crewmen, but no captain. With rigging and sails covered in ice, the ship was totally out of control. She missed colliding with the ferry, but in the Lower Bay ran into a three-masted schooner, which had anchored to ride out the gale. One of the *Heitman*'s crew jumped aboard the three-master, but before the others could follow, the two schooners had parted company and the *Heitman* was heading madly for the open ocean. Neither the *Mary Heitman* nor her four remaining crew members were ever seen again.

Ferry captains rammed their way across the ice-clogged water at full steam, but ice in the slips proved too much of an obstacle. The only way to get ashore was by jumping onto the ice and climbing to the pier on ladders. Several women made it along with the men, although they had to be boosted, carried, and hauled. After that unnerving experience, most of the women took a look at the street and decided to stay in the ferry-house. They would wait, they said optimistically, until the streets were plowed.

Commuters have always been subject to unpleasant surprises, but by and large they were getting better train service in 1888 than they are getting now. It was, therefore, with confidence that many commuters arrived at their local train stations on that blizzardy Monday morning. Those who came earliest found trains running, and some boarded them and arrived at their destination almost as usual. For example, William Franklin Draper, a Pennsylvania Railroad official whose office was in New York, had spent that weekend, as he usually did, in Philadelphia and had taken a Pennsylvania Railroad train for New York at midnight on Sunday. The train reached Jersey City, its terminal, at 6 A.M. An hour later, Draper left his Pullman car, breakfasted in the Jersey City station restaurant, boarded a ferryboat that was just leaving, and arrived in downtown Manhattan at eight. At the ferry station he found a cab, which took him to his office at Union Square, getting him there before nine. He later marveled that he had taken "the last train out of Philadelphia for three days, the last ferryboat (on time) for three days and the last cab (at a normal fare) for three days."

But such luck was not for everyone.

Ernest Baynes was a twenty-year-old student at the College of the City of New York (then on Lexington Avenue and 23rd Street). He lived in Westchester County and walked half a mile every day to catch a commuter train. Sometimes he ran all the way, which in those days was very unusual. He ran because he was in training for a footrace. When, early Monday morning,

67

no trains appeared at his usual station, Ernest decided to walk (and run) to school.

He set out, following the New Haven Railroad track. At West Farms, in the Bronx, he bought a newspaper and put it under his cap, for warmth. Soon after, the increasingly large drifts forced him to leave the track for the highway. Passing a stable, he begged a piece of string to tie his cap down, rested a few minutes, and pressed on. By now, the drifts on the road were waist-deep; he later learned that two men had died in the drifts on that road. He returned to the tracks and crossed a trestle by crawling all the way to keep from being blown off. At the end of the trestle he broke into an empty switch tender's box. There was a small shaving mirror on the wall, and Ernest took a look at himself. He saw that his face and ears were frozen and covered with a thick armor of frozen sleet and ice. This frightened him. The image of Hamlet's father came to mind. But since there was no possibility of turning back, he pressed on toward the city. Two switch tenders inside the next shelter called him in, thawed him out, and suggested he try to catch an el train. The early morning accident had shut down the Third Avenue line, but Ernest managed to board a Second Avenue train that very slowly got him to 42nd Street.

Since it was now afternoon, he decided to skip college. He stopped at a Western Union office to wire his parents not to worry, and then went to a friend's house on 44th Street. On Wednesday he returned to Westchester by hitching a ride on the first relief train to leave Grand Central. His wire did not arrive until the following Sunday.

Along the same commuter line, two older men had a more life-threatening time of it. Their train ran into a huge snowdrift soon after leaving Baychester at 7:35 and did not move again for three days. Most of the passengers waited in the train all day, burning coal from the tender in the car stoves. There was no food or drink on the train.

About 4 P.M., with the cars beginning to grow very cold, two friends, Henry W. Taft (a brother of the future president) and A. L. Hammett, decided to try to make it back to Baychester—just a mile and a half behind—hoping to hire a carriage or sleigh there to take them home. "As the day wore on, anxiety and physical discomfort crept rapidly upon us," wrote Taft later. "Coal in the tender and in the cars was soon exhausted," and the wind whistled through "the loose joints" of the wooden car.

They started off on foot, plodding down the track, and then, when they came to a long trestle, inching along on their hands and knees. With each gust of wind, they had to stop and cling to the ties in order not to be blown to their deaths in the rocky ravine below. During lulls, they got up and ran as fast as possible. Each drift took more of their failing strength, and when they crossed another trestle in the teeth of the wind, their ears and faces froze.

At Baychester, they could find no one willing to provide a conveyance at any price. On they trudged, taking the long way around Pelham Bay so as to avoid the nightmare of crawling over another trestle. They met no one, and it was getting dark. "The scene was weird and forbidding. Often we were forced to help each other out of drifts which were from five to ten feet high." Hammett began to grow dizzy, Taft said, "and fell into that mental state where he was indifferent. Feeling that he might succumb, I shared with him part of my depleted energies. He was thus enabled to continue. After covering a long trek of five miles in five strenuous and sometimes agonizing hours, we reached our village railroad station [Pelham]. The agent was aghast as we entered. Our faces were largely hidden under a coating of ice, and our eyelids were frozen open, leaving no protection to the eye from the biting sleet." By the time they reached home, "our eyes were closed by the weight of the ice and we staggered to and fro like drunken men."

On the Harlem Division of the New York Central, some commuter trains made the trip into town as far as Mott Haven (in the Bronx at East 138th Street). Here they had to stop, one behind another for miles, because the tracks into Grand Central station were heavily drifted and impassable.

One commuter marooned on that line was a wealthy social-ite, Frederick Van Wyck, bound for the city after a weekend at his country place in Scarsdale. "I told my coachman," Van Wyck wrote in his memoirs, "to have Odette, a nettlesome lass, ready to take me to the 6:47 train. Not realizing the condition of the weather, I pulled the bell and out of the stable came Odette on her hind legs. Under the evergreen tree she lunged, leaving the top of my buggy hanging in its branches. There it hung for three days. I scrambled into the buggy, or what was left of it, and . . . Odette took us to the station, giving all the warning possible by her naughty behavior, but we intelligent mortals took no heed that it was a terrific storm. Waiting in the station, not even the milk train due at 4 A.M. had passed and Twombly [Harrison McK. Twombly], son-in-law of W. H. Vanderbilt, was frantically telegraphing for milk for his children. About 8:15 a "train came limping along and off we went with many jerks and stops, engine and cars covered with snow and ice." At the next station, twenty minutes were lost while Twombly sent his useless telegrams. "On again at a snail's pace with our engine's last gasp at Mott Haven, at 12:15." Van Wyck and some friends got off and bought crackers and cheese at a nearby grocery. When they returned to the train, they learned that there were fifteen trains behind them.

Van Wyck then telegraphed his friend Chauncey Depew,

70

president of the New York Central and Hudson River Railroad, requesting to be rescued. By some fluke this message got through, and four hours later Van Wyck received a hand-carried reply. Depew said that he would try to send plenty of coal, but that there was no chance of any train reaching Grand Central that night. "This was the last we heard from the outside world until next day, as the engines were frozen where they stood."

Near the top of Manhattan Island was the Spuyten Duyvil railroad cut, 150 feet deep, 500 feet long, and curved. Known to railroaders as Spike, it had a bad reputation. If a train, for any reason, had to stop while running through it, the trains behind could not see what had happened, and signal systems were far from foolproof. It was probably fortunate that on that Monday morning the cut soon became heavily drifted, so that no trains could get into it. At 6:40 A.M., the Croton local, with seven commuter-filled coaches, hit a mountainous drift at the northern mouth of the cut and went no further. Behind it was the Peekskill local, with eight coaches, and behind that, two sleeper trains from the West. Soon eight trains—nearly a mile of trains—were stalled one behind the next, and there they remained for nearly three days.

Samuel M. Davis, telegraph operator on the Croton train, happened to live close by. He went home and set his wife and mother to making bread and coffee. From the neighborhood grocery he bought everything that could go into a sandwich, and when the bread was baked, the women made three hundred sandwiches and three big iron kettles of coffee. A hundred or more passengers had to share six crockery cups, but no one complained. Other kind souls fed them sporadically until Wednesday, when the cut was cleared by means of a snowplow, drawn by twenty-eight horses, and hundreds of men shoveling in front of it.

At noon on Monday, a Mr. Prescott and his wife left a train at Mott Haven and started walking downtown. "It was impossible to tell where the drifts lay, because of the many depressions in the road. . . . The snow was seldom less than knee-deep and while walking along in what appeared to be a level we would suddenly find ourselves floundering up to our armpits. My wife was almost chilled to death. The most of the time she was wading through snow up to her waist." Why did they leave the train? "Because we feared being frozen to death if we stayed there. Before we left the train the passengers were chopping up the card tables and seats for firewood. It was simply a question of staying and freezing or striking out and taking our chances of getting home. In fact, we did not think the traveling would prove so bad as it did."

A gentleman on a train stalled in New Jersey may have shown the best judgment of all. He got out of his car, intending to walk back to the station, but by the time he reached the other end of the car he reconsidered. He climbed back on the train and stayed there until he was rescued.

5

Stranded
Trains

THE GRAND CENTRAL DEPOT, fronting on 42nd Street, was a many-turreted red brick building in the Second Empire style, dating from 1871. Every day hundreds of trains arrived. After passing 125th street they entered a tunnel, emerged at 59th Street, and then by way of an open cut down Fourth Avenue (officially renamed Park Avenue in 1888) ended their journey in the Grand Central's train shed. This huge space had a glass roof and looked not unlike the shed at the Gare du Nord in Paris. It was the busiest railroad terminal on the continent. But on Monday, March 12 (as one of the New York *Sun*'s reporters wrote), "The interior of the station and the yard immediately outside, where the hissing of steam and the clanging of bells is heard day and night, were as silent as the grave. Clouds of snow were driven into the immense station, whirled up to the transparent ceiling, and again fell softly on the long lines of trains. . . . No sound was audible in the great structure save that of the moaning of the wind."

Of forty regular mail trains, only one came into Manhattan that day, the Chicago mail, six hours late. Three others, from Washington, Philadelphia, and Baltimore, arrived, like all trains from the south, at terminals in New Jersey, and the mail was sent across the Hudson by ferry. No more trains of any kind came into New Jersey terminals until Wednesday, and only one more arrived at Grand Central, the Boston express. This was a popular parlor-car train, which had left Boston, as it did every evening, at 10:30 P.M. With about 150 passengers in sleepers and coaches, the train had a clear run until it arrived at Hartford, at 2:41 A.M. Snow was beginning to fall there, and it was coming down very heavily by the time the express reached New Haven. At Stamford, a blizzard was evident. The cars were heated but apparently not well insulated, because the wind crept in through the cracks, causing the passengers to reach for their overcoats.

After Stamford, progress was made between jerky starts and sudden stops. The express was three hours late at the Harlem Bridge into Manhattan, and it stopped completely at 59th Street because of snowdrifts in the open cut. Shovelers took two hours to clear the drifts, and then a relief engine succeeded in pulling the train the remaining fifteen city blocks to Grand Central.

The Boston express was the last train to get through, and behind it many more sat helpless on the tracks. The Stamford local, stalled at 110th Street, was loaded with angry business-men and brokers. Having heard that the Boston express had been shoveled out, they were eager to know why they had not been. The brakeman was dispatched, with that question, on foot to Grand Central, a grueling walk along the tracks. But already the drifts were beyond control. A message came back: "The Officials have been endeavoring for some time to get an engine through the Fourth Avenue tunnel, but have found it now absolutely impossible." The railroad company ordered food to be sent to those who stayed on board, but several tycoons couldn't wait and hustled off on foot.

In the offices of the New York Central and Hudson River Railroad, at Grand Central depot, President Depew and his executives were beginning to realize that they had a major problem on their hands; but they had no idea of its extent because the telegraph wires were dead. Depew, who had succeeded the late William H. Vanderbilt as the railroad's president, was considered the brightest and best of Vanderbilt's top executives; but a day like Monday, March 12, 1888, tried his mettle. By late morning, it was clear that the railroad would either have to hire thousands of men to shovel snow or wait for the drifts to melt, since no plow had yet been invented that could deal adequately with large quantities of snow on a railroad track. Depew lost no time in sending out a call for labor. Because shoveling icy snow in a howling blizzard was one of the hardest and lowest paid of jobs, immmigrants straight from the ships were the most likely labor source. Not many years before, these would have been mostly Irish. Now they were nearly all Italian—unskilled, illiterate, but eager to work, and, most important, available in large numbers. They did not find work easily, because to American employers they seemed alarmingly foreign, with their total lack of English and their swarthy looks. Even the roughest Irishman, just off the boat, had always spoken some semblance of English.

It's an ill wind that blows nobody good, and the fierce winds of the blizzard blew jobs to the Italians. By afternoon, hundreds had been signed on and were at work on the tracks, even though the wind was piling up drifts faster than the workers could shovel them away. The superintendent of the railroad had the bright idea of taking them to the station dining room and laying on a hearty meal, which included spaghetti and red wine. The hope was that they would then go back to work with renewed strength and enthusiasm, but instead the effect was stupefying, particularly for those who had not had a large meal for some time or, perhaps, any meal at all. Many of them gave up after another hour's digging, and again the drifts had the best of it.

In defense of the workmen it must be said that the drifts they were tackling were as hard as icebergs. Shovels proved of little use, and the superintendent soon sent out a call for a thousand pickaxes. In an experiment, a drift was rammed with a locomotive, but the result was considerable damage to the locomotive and none at all to the drift.

Chauncey Depew, at his desk on Monday and Tuesday when many others in the executive offices were absent, received reporters, who remarked that he seemed surprisingly cheerful.

"This is all so overwhelming that nobody swears," he told them. "Everybody is good-natured. How about our road, you ask? Why, there isn't any road. The roads are all gone. We have not been able to do anything in the way of moving trains. Six hundred men are trying to clear out the tunnel between Fifty-ninth and Ninety-sixth and have made some progress. There is no way of telling when trains will move."

"And how many passengers are in the stalled trains?" a reporter asked.

"We have no way of knowing," Depew said regretfully. "We don't even know how many trains are stalled. The wires are down and we can't reach any of the station agents."

According to the *Sun*, "the pleasant frame of mind that characterized Mr. Depew was not shared by his subordinates." It was they who had to deal with the public and with waiting rooms crowded with short-tempered customers asking questions that could not be answered. "Mr. Depew admitted," the *Sun* went on, "that most of the unfortunates who were caught in the local trains were wealthy brokers and businessmen, and smiled sadly as he thought of the wrath that would come down upon him and his fellow officials from these patrons of his road."

After the reporters left, a man burst into Depew's office and said he'd paid his fare to ride to Grand Central from Yonkers, but had had to walk from Spuyten Duyvil. He wanted his money back. Depew quickly bade him good morning and had him removed. The president of the New York Central was a perfect gentleman, an after-dinner wit, and a favorite of the ladies, but he had not become a protégé of the Vanderbilts or president of their railroad for any of those reasons. He was also tough, unsentimental, and ruthless. After William H. Vanderbilt told a reporter "The public be damned," he realized how that looked in print and denied he'd said it. Depew was shrewd enough not to say it, but he was in the railroad business to make money and he certainly was not going to start refunding fares.

In the early days of railroading, signals were given by holding up fingers, waving flags or colored lanterns, showing hand-held "target" paddles, and keeping a sharp eye out. At the time of the Blizzard of '88, thousands of miles of American railroads were still being run the old-fashioned way (and some are even today).

Railroad employees were often on duty for longer hours than other workingmen, and on occasion, they worked steadily for several days. The colloquial expression "asleep at the switch," referring to an inattentive person, had a grim origin in nineteenth-century train wrecks. Little naps at the switch or the throttle could be fatal.

Pay on the railroads was low, although no lower than for many other types of manual labor. The men whose job it was to couple and uncouple cars were in constant danger. At least one was killed or cruelly maimed on an average of once a week. On freight trains, the brakemen had to work on top of the boxcars, controlling the brakes by spinning a wheel. If they were not very careful, they could be knocked from the roof by a low bridge or blown off by a strong wind. During the blizzard, a brakeman on the Boston and Providence Railroad, whose name, ironically, was Snow, was thrown to his death because the blinding snowstorm prevented him from seeing a low bridge. The railroad sent flowers to the funeral and a note of condolence to the widow, but nothing else. Mr. Snow should have been more careful.

A conductor on a train that stalled in the blizzard near Morristown, New Jersey, had his feet frozen while walking to get help and was incapacitated for life. Nothing was done for him either. Of course, in some instances, employers were more charitable, but government-required compensation was still many decades in the future.

On a train stuck near Westbury, Long Island, the engineer got out to go for help and was carried back to the train unconscious. A woman who saw this said, "there seems to be a sort of pride with them in keeping their engines alive, and all night they worked." Next morning, the conductor and others from the train procured a sleigh and blankets for the ladies, tucked them in snugly, and pulled them (without a horse) to Westbury.

Indeed there was "a sort of pride" in being a railroader, even in the lowest echelons. A fireman aboard a train detained by a huge drift near Danbury, Connecticut, later said, "I had no money and I was without food from Sunday until Tuesday. My task was to shovel snow from the coal in the tender and keep the fire and steam up. I was alone during Monday night, with the snow ten feet high all around. When dawn came, the engineer began to back the engine a few paces and ran it full-steam into that mountain of snow. The snow would all fall down on us and on the coal, and then we would use the shovels—the short-handled type was all we had. We kept this up until we reached Brewster, a distance of about four miles. That night I slept on a bench in the station, and some of the Italians who were shoveling gave me my first meal of Italian bread and bologna, the first time I ever had any."

A satellite view of the northeastern states late Monday would have revealed a vast white wilderness, with cities and villages only half-visible, and hundreds of wormlike black specks that were stalled railroad cars. Among the latter were four crack trains, such as the New York to Chicago midnight express, brought to an ignominious standstill fifty-seven miles west of Philadephia. A thirty-car freight train was derailed and thrown from an embankment near Reading, Pennsylvania; the private car of the noted Polish actress, Mme. Modjeska, was stranded somewhere near Wilkes-Barre; and countless humble day coaches were dead on backcountry short lines with long sonorous names, such as the Meriden, Waterbury, and Connecticut River; the Clove Valley and Catskill Mountain; or the St. Johnsbury and Lake Champlain. The fate of these trains and their passengers and crews varied considerably according to the ingenuity of conductors and engineers, the availability of makeshift heating arrangements and meals, and the eagerness of railroad owners to be helpful.

A Shore Line express from Boston to New York left Monday morning at 9:30 with two drawing-room cars, two coaches, a smoker, and a baggage car. The weather in Boston was disagreeable—sleety and windy—but not seriously worse than March days often are. In Rhode Island there was more rain than sleet. The express picked up passengers at Providence and continued its run, more or less on time. The first inkling of trouble ahead came at Kingston, Rhode Island. The newsboys there had no New York newspapers and were saying that no eastbound train had come through for hours.

West of Kingston, the rain began to fall in torrents. The train got across the Thames River at New London on its usual ferry (a bridge was not built there until 1889), and at the New London station the locomotive was replaced by two others that were stronger and heavier. About ten miles farther, along the open waterfront at Niantic, everything was sleet, which soon turned to blinding snow, driven by a very strong gale. About a mile beyond Saybrook station, the train stuck fast in a cut filled with snow. As the Providence *Journal* reported later, "They worked and tugged to get out, but the heavy driving wheels of the engines spun around on the tracks like buzzsaws and could not bite the track." The struggle was abandoned after fifteen minutes, and a strange silence fell. There sat the ninety-five passengers, looking out at snow falling so thickly that the rocky walls of the cut were barely visible to them.

The conductor was in command (as he still is on today's trains), with even the engineer under his orders. Aboard this train, the conductor was a Mr. deWolfe. Although recently arisen from a sickbed, he elected to walk back to Saybrook station to see about help. When he got there, two or three hours later, "both of his ears were frozen and if the distance had been half a mile longer he would have perished in the snow. He was barely able to crawl when he reached the station platform. He was assisted by people there, and his frozen ears were packed in snow," the standard treatment at the time.*

Meanwhile, those still on the train began to worry about him. Others tried to walk back to Saybrook, but abandoned the attempt and counted themselves lucky to find the train again. Finally, about eleven o'clock Monday night, deWolfe returned to his train, bringing the following tidings: there was no possible chance of getting help from Saybrook; the company had not authorized him to hire men to dig the train out, and it would be useless anyway until the storm ceased; and, no, he could not get them anything to eat, because he was afraid the company "would not allow his bills."

At this, the passengers forgot their concern for deWolfe's sufferings and began belaboring him with their anger and frustration. They were not yet starving, but they had eaten up everything on the train except a few crackers, and were keenly interested in where the next meal was coming from. "The car was warm and tight, but the air began to be very heavy and oppressive. It was like a tomb."

Although food was lacking, there turned out to be plenty of whiskey, and among the coach passengers were singers and dancers of the Ideal Opera Company. Those in the coaches were described later as "a jolly lot. . . . The poorest attempt at a joke won applause, and the passengers were determined to make the most of the dubious prospects." But the drawing-room-car passengers were not amused and described the coach goings-on as "a midnight brawl." They locked themselves into their car, grumbled, and tried to sleep. One young lady was heard to exclaim, "If only I could take my bustle off!" That she

*According to modern medicine, the effective cure for frostbite is rapid rewarming in a water bath whose temperature is controlled at between 100 and 108 degrees. Rubbing, particularly with snow, only makes things worse.

should speak of her bustle in public shows to what extremes
these people were being driven.

As soon as dawn broke, some of the gentlemen left the train
to look for farmhouses where food might be bought or scrounged.
They were successful, and soon afterward other farmers in the
vicinity got the word and brought boiled eggs, pork sandwiches, cake, coffee, and milk. "A nibble here and a nibble
there all day Tuesday" kept the passengers going. The belea-
guered conductor made his way back to Saybrook and this
time, somehow, got authority to employ some shovelers.

"Work was begun at once and continued but a short time,
as the drifting snow filled in as fast as thrown out. One hour
was enough to demonstrate that this was energy thrown away.
The snow in places was up to the body of the cars, but the train
stood out of the ocean of whiteness like a monument." Local
people came to rubberneck and to invite passengers to come
home with them for the night. Some went. Others spent a
second night in the train, even though the air was worse than
ever, and the soft coal burning in the car stoves had covered
them all with greasy soot.

On Wednesday morning, a few walked to Saybrook. "The
travelling was terrible and exhausting. In some parts of the road
one could walk on the crust of the snow, and in other and
numerous places the traveller sank to his waist in the treacher-
ous substance." At about 9:30 A.M. those remaining on board
were surprised to observe two gentlemen in fur coats and hats,
toiling their way on foot toward the train. The gallant rescuers
were a Mr. Harris, of Providence, who, the newspapers said,
was "in search of a young woman," and another gentleman,
name not given, from Salem, who wished to succor his sister,
her two children, and the children's nurse, all of whom had
been headed for Florida.

The two had somehow made their way to New London by train, sleigh, and boat, and had then chartered a tug that took them along the shore of Long Island Sound, seventeen miles by water from New London and only a few miles from the stalled train. When other passengers learned about the tug, they clamored to go with them, and the two gentlemen agreed to take up to twenty, if they would share the cost of the charter. The trek to Saybrook was described later as extremely unpleasant. With the women in their trailing dresses, and the children, they had to cross a long trestle "that looked insecure for foot." Snow was no longer falling, but the wind still blew wildly. From Saybrook the party reached Saybrook Point and their tugboat by means of a one-car train on the Valley Railroad, a short line whose tracks happened to be passable.

Next day, the Providence *Journal* wrote scoldingly, "it seems that the company intends to run no more danger, but let the travelling public work out its own salvation." The following week, some of the passengers corroborated this judgment in letters to the papers: they had had to survive on crackers, the tugboat party had been asked to pay for food at the Saybrook Station, no free tickets back to Boston or Providence were offered—or, indeed, any other kind of help, and one lady's jewels had been stolen while she slept. The stalled train was at last hauled to New Haven on Thursday evening, and those who wished were put aboard a Sound steamer for New York.

One indignant Saybrook man wrote to contradict the cracker story. The people of Saybrook and environs, he said, had fed the passengers lavishly. One man alone (perhaps the writer?) had brought them a hundred hot biscuits, a hundred sausages, and a hundred boiled eggs, not to mention pickles, canned meat, coffee, and milk. And others had plied them with pie, cake, soup, chicken, and much else. Should another train ever be stalled at Saybrook, he finished, "the engine will not be alone in 'whistling' for assistance."

These sagas of stalled trains were repeated again and again —some happier, some more pathetic. On a Providence and Worcester train, stalled when the locomotive jumped the track, the conductor somehow managed to feed his passengers through the night with pie, doughnuts, and coffee. Aboard the Delaware, Lackawanna and Western (known to some patrons as "the Delay, Linger, and Wait), somewhere in New Jersey, an investigation of the baggage car turned up a crate of eggs, two barrels of bread, and a firkin of butter. The ladies boiled the eggs on the parlor-car stove.

Passengers on trains that were carrying theatrical companies had the most fun: free performances up and down the aisles, including one by a troupe of actors touring in a play called *Lost in the Snow*. On a train with no heat, a dance troupe kept their fellow travelers warm and happy by teaching them the tarantella. Mme. Modjeska, snug in her palace car, suffered no ill effects from being stranded for three days, except that she missed some performances, along with her cut of the box office receipts.

Aboard a local in upper New York State, a member of the state legislature put on a show of his own, after "punishing" a few whiskies. He clogged wildly up and down the aisle, singing minstrel songs at the top of his lungs. The newspapers kindly refrained from identifying him.

6

"The Land Is an Ocean of Snow"

"IN TRUTH the land is an ocean of snow," wrote an Albany *Journal* reporter, embarking on a blizzard story for the Monday evening paper. And, in truth, he was in the deepest part of it: between Monday and Wednesday up to fifty inches of snow fell in and near Albany, as well as in southern Vermont and New Hampshire, the Berkshires, and western Connecticut. He went on, "Albany was almost as remote from the outside world this morning as though the methods of a hundred years ago were still in vogue. . . . The streets resembled rolling country. . . . The city looked dead and was literally buried." No horsecars, no carriages, no wagon teams could he see, as he gazed from the high window of his newspaper in the middle of town; and the few people walking "looked like flies in a sugarbowl."

In the State Senate in Albany, only seven out of fifty legislators reported for work. After about an hour they adjourned and departed, leaving behind for posterity a record of lame-brained palaver:

SENATOR SLOAN: I had not intended to speak on this subject but I must remark that the snowfall is a heavy one.

SENATOR MCNAUGHTON: It is a very serious matter. What is to become of all this snow? I look for unprecedented freshets.

CLERK HALL: It beats the Dutch, don't it?

Desperate for news, small, isolated papers like the *Journal* printed alarming rumors: a big fire at Stamford had left the railroad station in ashes and most of the town on fire; nine pilot schooners out of New York Harbor had been sunk; the Brighton Hotel at Coney Island had blown into the ocean taking guests and staff with it; a Sound steamer had gone aground near New Haven, and the survivors had frozen to death on the beach.

None of these calamities turned out to have happened. Only gradually did the true fatalities become known. There were hundreds of them, and most were lonely deaths by freezing or accident. An elderly black man, a peddler of faggots, froze to death in a snowdrift as he tried to reach his shack on the outskirts of Middletown, Connecticut . . . Elsewhere in the state, a laundress, carrying a heavy load of wash, slipped on the ice, broke her leg, and died because no one heard her cries . . . A man in Milltown, New Jersey, went out to get a doctor for his sick wife. He lost his way and froze to death, and when someone finally reached his house, his wife was dead in her bed and his small children were starving . . . Three young men who worked at the Singer factory in Perth Amboy, New Jersey, crossed to Staten Island in a rowboat. By some miracle they reached shore, but died trying to find their way home across a field. All three were found a week later, frozen to death in a haystack where they had taken refuge . . . These unrelated tragedies would have made big headlines had they happened all at once in one place. Individually, they were not the major stories reporters hope for, and so our man in Albany burbled on:

As the blizzard went into its second day, the papers rushed to print news of it, not sparing words like "panic," "terror," and "paralyzed." This is the front page of the New York *Morning Journal*'s Blizzard Extra.

This fine photograph (left), showing fallen wires, impassable snow drifts, and bewildered citizens, was taken in lower Manhattan, looking toward Wall Street.
Museum of the City of New York

Blizzard humor: A sign erected on a tunneled snow-drift reads "This Way to Canada." *Museum of the City of New York*

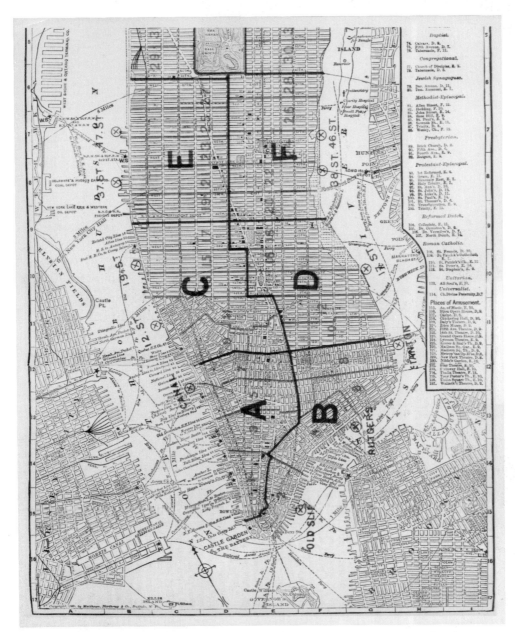

A plan of lower Manhattan in 1888 shows the docks and the amazingly numerous ferry lines. (The large letters refer to street-cleaning operations.) *The New-York Historical Society*

On Tuesday, March 13, the East River near the Brooklyn Bridge was completely blocked by ice floes. Hundreds crossed on the ice between Brooklyn and Manhattan, including the intrepid group shown here. *Museum of the City of New York*

A Brooklyn sidewalk scene, just after the storm. *The Brooklyn Museum*

Winds gusting to fifty miles an hour swept through open spaces like Union Square and bowled over pedestrians. Women, with their cumbersome skirts and hats, suffered the most. *The New-York Historical Society*

During the blizzard, helpful policemen went about the New York streets trying to restore circulation to the frozen ears and noses of hapless pedestrians by rubbing them with snow. No doubt this brought psychological comfort, but modern doctors would say it was useless, even harmful.
The New-York Historical Society

Chauncy M. Depew, president of
the blizzard-stalled New York Central and Hudson Railroad.
Museum of the City of New York

Former Senator Roscoe Conkling, a
blizzard victim, is caricatured here
as a turkey cock. One of his enemies, Senator James G. Blaine,
had referred in a speech to Conkling's "majestic, super-eminent,
overpowering turkey-gobbler strut."
The New-York Historical Society

Abram S. Hewitt, mayor of New
York during the blizzard, a self-
made merchant, was elected to office
in 1886 on a Democratic reform
platform. He defeated both Theodore Roosevelt, a Republican, and
the left-leaning Labor candidate,
Henry George.
Museum of the City of New York

A heavily storm-damaged schooner, at Lewes, Delaware. *Delaware State Archives*

It took three steam locomotives, plus an improvised plow rigged on a cow-catcher, plus shovelers, to open the main railroad line between New Haven and Hartford. Here, the locomotives enter Meriden, Connecticut. *Turner Railroad Collection, Connecticut Historical Society*

Pittsfield, Massachusetts: Snowed in. *The Berkshire Eagle*

Pittsfield, Massachusetts: The drifts turn to floods. Similar scenes took place on main streets all over the Northeast.
The Berkshire Eagle

"A young woman was seen ploughing her way up Beaver to Eagle . . . with cheeks a rose red and heart thumping like a steam engine she leaned against the telephone pole and waited to regain her equilibrium. Meanwhile the telephone pole swayed in quick sympathy with her thumping heart and the occasional passserby envied that telephone pole."

On the whole, small-town and country people fared better, even in fifty inches of snow, than those in the big cities. They were not at the mercy of a system out of control but could deal individually with the storm, as they had been taught to do by parents and grandparents. If they were provident and prudent, they had ample food put away in the cellar: bins of potatoes and turnips and flour; meat hanging on hooks or salted pork in barrels; stacked jars of preserved fruits and vegetables; and plenty of dandelion wine and apple cider. They could stay put until the weather lifted. They were also well supplied with heavy clothing and boots and, sometimes, snowshoes; and the woodshed would be stacked with firewood. Even in a farm-house completely buried in snow, a family could survive for days in a dim twilight, receiving fresh air only through the chimneys. A pig farmer in Tidewater Virginia, finding the ground floor of his house flooded, took his pigs and his wife upstairs, and together they sat out the storm. Unless someone was in need of a doctor, or the roof blew off, the chief concern of country people was to maintain a path to the barn so that they could feed and water the stock. Near Mahopac Falls, New York, a farmwife, whose husband was laid up in bed and whose children were too young to help, cut steps in one side of a big snowdrift that lay between the barn and the house. She climbed up that side and rolled down the other, and so was able to reach her twenty-seven cows, night and morning, all through the blizzard.

In the snowiest part of southern Vermont, a young school-master saw each of his children home, herding them along tied together with clothesline. The snow stung their faces "like birdshot," and once or twice he let them stop and lie down for a minute in the shelter of a fence. Having delivered each child safely, he went home and, after a short rest, dug two hundred feet to the barn, milked the cows, and fed them. It was three weeks before classes resumed and before he or anyone in that remote mountain place saw the face of an outsider.

For dwellers in the backcountry, 1888 might as well have been 1788 or 1688—except for oil lamps and wood-burning stoves. Railroad stations lost their usefulness, and, anyway, many villages were nowhere near one. A few miles marked the limit of most rural lives. Yet all of this would change within the lifetime of those children who, as the storm rolled toward them on Sunday, March 11, sat around a big dining table, their attention firmly focused on the roast that Father was carving.

Near the village of Montville, Connecticut, in the Thames River valley, the Chapell family awoke on Monday morning to the falling snow, and they recognized the signs of an extraordinary storm. Farmer Chapell, paterfamilias, had spent the night half a mile across the fields, at the home of his sick mother, who was asking for her children. His wife, at home, felt no alarm—she knew how to deal with big storms. Early in the morning, she sent her two elder boys, George and Alfred, to dig the essential path to the barn. Later, she dispatched George, a hulking sixteen-year-old, across the fields to Grandma's house with calf's-foot tea for the invalid. But then the unexpected happened: George returned, saying that Father had come down with a fever and couldn't get home, and would Mother please come.

Farm families always dreaded the unexpected, which destroyed their cautious plans. But Mrs. Chapell could see no alternative to leaving the four boys on their own: if her husband had sent for her, she must go.

By afternoon, Gurdon, nine, and little Legrand, four, had exhausted the amusements of the farm kitchen. They had popped corn and eaten it all, and they had fought over toys, and teased the cat. George was sulky at having to play nursemaid, and while Alfred was out at the barn, he decided to walk over to Grandma's and see how things were. The younger ones begged to come, but George shook his head. "You stay right here and behave yourselves," he said.

The kitchen clock ticked, the fire crackled, and the icy blizzard snow tapped the windows. Legrand and Gurdon were not used to such a quiet house, and it made them uneasy.

"What can we do?" asked Legrand.

"I know," Gurdon said recklessly. "We'll go and surprise Mother and Father."

They wrapped up warmly, as they had been taught. But when they stepped outside, they found a world they had never seen before. Usually, Grandma's house was in plain sight, two fields and a pasture away. Today, even the gateposts of their yard had disappeared. But Gurdon, a determined youngster, caught sight of a familiar elm tree, which he knew was in the direction they wanted to go. Seizing his brother's mittened hand, he set out.

George, having reached his grandmother's house with great difficulty, decided to spend the night. When Alfred returned from his chores and found no one home, he concluded that all three boys had left together. It was not until next morning, when the snow stopped for a while and Alfred drove the sleigh to the other house, that the little ones were discovered to be missing.

It took scarcely an hour for the entire neighborhood to assemble to look for them. So much snow had fallen since Monday afternoon that there were no tracks, but someone found Legrand's cap and mittens near an enormous drift.

"There's a stone wall under here," someone said. "The drift's higher'n the wall."

An old man suggested that they use bean poles to poke exploratory holes in the snow. To demonstrate, he stuck his staff into the drift.

"Ouch!" came a faint voice.

Frantically, everyone began burrowing into the drift and in a few minutes uncovered Gurdon, in a cave of snow, with his little brother, unconscious, leaning against him. They had been there for twenty-two hours.

The children were carried into the Chapells' warm kitchen. Mrs. Chapell seized her youngest son and sat down with him close to the stove. One of the neighbors, a seafaring man who had been in the Arctic, advised taking the child into a cool room and bathing him in tepid water. Both children were so stiff that their clothes had to be cut from them and their mouths pried open to receive doses of whiskey. Someone else insisted that each child must be wrapped in a sheet smeared thickly with molasses.

The two children survived not only their sojourn in the snowdrift but also the resuscitative treatments, and lived to old age. Legrand never forgot his brother's words, as they clung together under the snow: "We'll never get out of here. We will die, but I can't go and leave you alone and I can't carry you!" They were only two hundred feet from their grandmother's doorstep.

Everywhere, funerals and burials were interfered with. In Shelton, Connecticut, the Dibble family assembled for the funeral of a young woman who had died in childbirth. The services and burial were to have taken place on Monday, but no one, living or dead, was able to leave the house until Thursday.

On that day, neighbors got through with a "long box sleigh" and took the corpse to the cemetery. The funeral was finally held on Sunday. Meantime, the motherless infant was thriving, due to the providential stranding at the Dibble house of a milkman with a large can of milk.

Country people whom Providence failed to help often helped themselves by ingenious improvisations. Near Hartford, a Mrs. Brusselais found herself with twelve storm refugees in her house and no dinner to give them. Gathering up the frozen sparrows in her dooryard, she defrosted them and made them into a pie.

In Poughkeepsie, New York, Newell L. Davids, head salesman at the Great Atlantic and Pacific Tea Company, arrived at his store after lunch on Monday and found a drift in front of it so huge that no one could get in. He therefore dug out the drift to make what he called a snow house. It was twelve feet high, "tall enough inside, after it was dug out, for any person to walk without having to stoop." To his snowhouse he dug a connecting tunnel through another drift, from one side of the street to the other. His was one of only a few stores in Poughkeepsie that did business during the blizzard.

In New Haven, the telephone company put up its hello girls on Monday night at the city's best hotel, the Tremont House. Factory owners, it appears, were less maternal than Great-grandma Bell, but most of them allowed female employees to spend the night, supperless, lying on their workbenches. In Derby, Connecticut, thirty factory girls struggling homeward had to be rescued, close to death, from drifts by volunteer patrols.

Among New England cities, New Haven seems to have had the most difficult time of it. THE MOST TERRIFIC STORM EVER WITNESSED IN THIS LATITUDE was the headline in the New Haven *Register*, as soon as it could get to press.

On Monday evening, "the city was in total darkness except where a few gas lights burned, and looked like a southern city after the Union troops had visited it and a battle fought." Besides losing its lights, all its telegraph wires, and most of its telephone service—not to mention a large number of ships damaged in the harbor or beached along the nearby shores— New Haven suffered various kinds of minor distress. A pie wagon overturned in a drift. Horse and wagon escaped without much damage, but "the same cannot be said for the pastry." Five Yale students were arrested for throwing snowballs. Fines amounted to as much as fifteen dollars apiece and costs. "Some think that the fine was altogether too extensive," the *Register* noted. "Others are of the opinion that the boys escaped with a light penalty and didn't get half enough."

Boston received less snow than rain and sleet, but nevertheless all telegraphic communication, with the exception of one line to Worcester and the cable to London, was knocked out. Messages to Washington went by a roundabout route: Boston to London, London to Chicago, and Chicago to Washington.

"It is fifty years since Boston has been so affected by a storm," one outgoing message read, adding that no trains were running, there was a terrific sea beating upon the coast, "and but for the long-distance telephone Boston would be as far removed from the rest of the world . . . as if it were situated in the desert of Sahara."

But it took more than a giant blizzard to alarm the editor of the Narragansett *Times*, a tiny weekly published in southern Rhode Island. On the Friday following the blizzard, the paper carried its usual load of local news about births, marriages, deaths, and stolen horses, and noted also that there had been something of a snowstorm and "horrible traveling" all week.

The disturbance had also seriously interfered with lobster traps. Nevertheless, added the editor, this storm had not been as bad as people were saying; he was sure he remembered a worse one when he was a boy. And, looking on the bright side, the bad weather had driven the birds out of the woods and he had seen a rose-breasted grosbeak.

In the Catskill Mountains, the wind was particularly high. It blew the roof off the railroad station in Liberty, New York, and the chimney off a nearby house. "We had to put out the fires," the owner reported, "wrap ourselves in blankets and comfortables and walk the floor all night, expecting any minute that the house would blow down on us."

In Philadelphia, a brand-new iron smokestack, 140 feet high, crashed to the ground. So did flagpoles, plate-glass windows, and roofs. A druggist walking past a police station was suddenly seized by the wind, as if by an avenging angel, and hustled through its door. He came to rest in front of the sergeant's desk. At a suburban railroad station on the Main Line, a boy who sold papers and candy was blown off the platform into the path of an oncoming train. Someone saw it happen and alerted the engineer just in time. Rescued, the boy was desolate because he had lost his hat and a basket of candies.

In Baltimore, the very low tide grounded oceangoing ships at their docks and prevented immigrant ships from debarking their passengers. To get the immigrants ashore was impossible, nor was anyone ready to process them when they got there. Without the telegraph, Baltimore officials reverted to an antiquated system of sending messages from one old watchtower to another by means of signal lamps. Repairmen were out in the storm all night trying to restore the downed wires—slow, difficult, and dangerous work. Further south, on Chesapeake Bay, the water was at the lowest level on record. "No vessel could live in the bay Sunday night," said an oldtime Chesapeake sailor. Most of the craft were driven ashore, suffering serious damage or total loss. At least forty seamen died, half of them on oyster dredgers that capsized or were cast upon the beaches.

News from Washington flashed to the world by way of one wire to Chicago. "The halls of Congress," one dispatch said, "were occupied by a sparse attendance of the most daring of its members." The subject under discussion in the House was a protectionist bill and, in the Senate, fishing rights, "dull as ditchwater."

7

On Foot

IN NEW YORK CITY the daytime sky was so dark that it was hard to tell when true dusk began to fall. Businesses closed early and sent their employees home or, rather, into the streets, for no one had any idea how home was to be reached. The horsecars had clearly collapsed, but as ferries and a few el trains were rumored to be operating, many people trudged off to try their luck. Those with plenty of money in their pockets attempted to find cabs; those who failed, as most did, turned to hailing the few wagons that passed, offering to pay handsomely for rides. But even as much as fifty dollars, the equivalent of a month's earnings, was not enough for most drivers.

An exception was a young man named J. H. Meyer, who drove a caterer's wagon delivering the pickles, sauerkraut, bread, cold meats, and so on, that saloons offered gratis to bar customers. Early in the day he abandoned his normal rounds and devised a free enterprise of his own, giving short rides at exorbitant fees. At the end of the day he drove the horse to the stable and walked home, his pockets full of bills. The catch was that he was in bed for four weeks with frozen feet and lost his job.

The proprietors of a paint store on the Bowery, Henry Toch and his cousin Luke, were fortunate in owning "an old Rockaway carriage which had been in our family for years and was at that time in the stable. We had two strong faithful horses who did truck service." And a driver. All three of them proceeded along in the shelter of the el, but after two hours, they had progressed only about a dozen blocks. "The horse's body was practically buried in snow from the bottom up, and we felt as though the old rig would break to pieces." The Toch cousins got out and walked home, a mile-long journey that took them three hours. The driver followed the el tracks back to the stable.

If cabs were to be found at all in the downtown area, it was likely to be in front of the Astor House, one of the city's best hotels. According to the New York *Sun*, "the struggle for carriages was very exciting. The starter and the colored boss porter in the corridor were subjected to all sorts of blandishments by the applicants."

One gentleman who hailed a cabbie and asked, "How much to 42nd Street?" was told, "A hundred dollars."

"I'm not trying to buy the outfit," the gentleman protested.

"That may be," said the cabbie, "but this old nag and I have been good friends for many years, so it would take all of that and more to induce me to expose him to such weather. Good-bye, Sir. The old horse and I are going to the barn."

People who were determined to reach home that night soon realized that the surest way to get there was to walk. "Broadway was the most popular track," noted the *Sun*, "and a black procession of pedestrians soon marched along its more sheltered western sidewalk. It was laborious work, the wind being dead ahead and laden with cold, fine snow, as well as keener and harder particles off the roofs." Many of the bravest walkers of the morning faltered at the thought of the return. "It was not alone the difference between a fair wind and a head wind. The lameness and fatigue resulting from the unaccustomed and vigorous work of the down trip was the chief trouble."

Among a few plucky women who set out to walk home was May Morrow, an eighteen-year-old telegrapher for a small wholesale chemical business who lived at a boardinghouse on West 47th Street near Tenth Avenue. By leaving home very early that morning and catching a Ninth Avenue elevated train, she had arrived at her Front Street office only a few minutes late. No one else turned up except the head of the firm, Mr. Garrigues. Furthermore, since the wires were dead, there was little for her to do. When she looked out of the window she could see hundreds of telegraph and electricity and telephone wires lying in a tangle all over the street. Some of the poles had been snapped in two by the wind or pushed into dangerously slanting positions; others had crashed through windows. The wires hissed and writhed like snakes as they lay on the ground, and passersby gave them a wide berth. Once May heard the terrified neighing of a horse and, running to the window, saw a cab horse with wires encircling his neck. Before he could be released, he was dead.

Soon after the noon hour, Mr. Garrigues urged May not to try to reach home but to spend the night in the office. Then he left for his own home in the West 40s, telling her that he intended to catch the nearby Cortlandt Street ferry to Jersey City and then ride another ferry back to 42nd Street. "But that would be too cold and risky for a young lady," he said. "Better to stay where it's warm and dry." The office was not modern enough for steam heat, but it had a reliable woodstove and plenty of fuel.

Still, when May found herself alone in the dim gaslight, with daylight waning outside, she decided that she hated staying there. The Wall Street district was deserted at night, and it seemed to her that she would be the only living creature in a terrifying world of storm. She removed her bustle and locked it into a file cabinet. Then she pinned up her skirt to the level of her boot tops, hoping that anyone who saw her would be too busy with the storm to notice—for only prostitutes wore their skirts so high. She tied her hat on firmly with package string, and protected her ankles and chest with newspapers. Her stout boots were still wet from the morning's journey, but there was no way to dry them. Her coat had a waist-length cape, then the fashion, which offered extra warmth for her shoulders.

Then she set out. First she went through the arcade in the nearby Equitable Life Assurance Building, gaining a block's worth of shelter; but at the other end the wind spun her around leaving her dazed. A stout man, in rubber boots and a fur coat, suddenly appeared in her path.

"Stop a minute, young lady," he said. "Your ears are freezing."

One thing a New York working girl knew, having been told it a hundred times, was that she must not converse with strange men, no matter how avuncular they might appear. Strange men, it seemed, made a habit of ingratiating themselves with young girls in order to "carry them away." How this was done or whither they were carried, May did not know and had never inquired. Young girls were not supposed to know more than they had to for survival. Even this much information was given only to girls whom poverty obliged to go out alone in the world. To ask further questions would be to hint at impurity of mind.

"Let me pass, Sir," May said grimly to the man. And she hurried on.

Two blocks further on, another man steered her into a doorway and, before she could scream, began to rub her ears.

"People don't realize when their ears are being frosted," he said.

May put her hand on one ear and felt nothing. That frightened her more than the man did. He was middle-aged, with kind and rather amused blue eyes.

"Where are you going?" he asked.

But, of course, she knew better than to tell him.

"Well, anyway," he said, "you'd better take care of your ears." And he arranged the cape of her coat over her head, patted her on her shoulder, and sent her on her way.

As she struggled up Broadway she observed that passersby often spoke to each other—sometimes with loud complaints about the weather, sometimes making jokes, sometimes simply exchanging greetings in a jolly manner. Something about sharing the hardships of the storm made people more friendly, and when a young man helped her across an icy street and asked, "Cold enough for you, Miss?" she even offered him a prim smile and said it was.

From May's office to where the numbered streets began added up to some thirty blocks. At that point, May still faced forty-seven more blocks uptown and then three long ones west to Tenth Avenue. She decided to stay on Broadway because there were more pedestrians there, and she got across the howling wilderness of Union Square by joining a single file of people holding on to each other's shoulders.

On her way, she saw some terrible sights. A man lay with his arms around the base of a lamppost, and she heard a policeman say, "He ain't drunk. He's dead."

A few blocks farther on, a little beggar girl, dressed in rags and clutching a basket, was being dug from a snowdrift.

"Where do you live, little girl?" a kind man was asking. "I will take you home."

The child began sobbing. "I can't go home. I got nothin' in my basket."

Near Union Square, May saw an elderly man fall in the

99

street and hit his head against something half-buried in snow. He got up again gamely, with a bloodied head.

"A horse's hoof! That was a horse's hoof I fell against," he announced loudly to anyone who would listen. "Kicked by a dead horse, by cracky!"

May noticed other walkers turning in at coffee shops and bars. There was more than the usual number of drunks on the street, and a strong smell of spirits every time she passed a saloon entrance. But May trudged on. She had no money except her usual dime for carfare, and, of course, she would not ask for any. She passed the darkened and closed-up stores on the "Ladies' Mile," the stretch of Broadway between 17th and 23rd streets: there were Lord and Taylor, Arnold Constable, Brooks Brothers, and other elegant shops she had never been in, all selling goods the likes of which she had never even been close to. Her eye was caught, as she hurried past, by ruby and diamond earrings, glinting in a jeweler's window, and at Lord and Taylor she noted a pale plaster arm, up to its elbow in a many-buttoned, white kid glove.

A shopgirl joined her for a few blocks.

"Stood all day at the counter and only sold one spool of thread," she told May. "Most girls didn't sell nothin'."

In Madison Square, she and the shopgirl walked backward, the wind was so fierce. They would have liked a few minutes' rest inside the doors of the nice hotels there; but good girls must never just stand anywhere or people might wonder about them.

After Madison Square, Broadway changed character. Here were many theaters, but almost none of them showed signs of life. The blinding arc lights that customarily lighted the streets in this area were dark tonight, and one did not hear the peculiar clicking and clacking sound they always made. The streets were unnaturally quiet.

Where Broadway crosses Seventh Avenue and 42nd Street, the future Times Square, May left the other girl and turned west to Ninth Avenue. Walking north under the el tracks, she could sometimes contrive to stay behind a tall person and use him as a windbreak. At West 47th Street, she perceived that the north side, where her boardinghouse was, had become impassable. She could hardly see the parlor windows of the brownstone row, let alone the stoops. Slipping and sliding and summoning strength she had not known she had, she walked the length of the south side of the block, crossed over, and floundered back two or three houses to her own address.

Her fellow boarders were watching for her, and some of them rushed out to help her into the house. She was nearly fainting, and the landlady put her to bed with a good dose of whiskey—the standard cure-all. After sixteen hours of sleep she began to feel normal and was back at work on Wednesday, not to miss an office day for the next forty years. In her late twenties, she married her boss (not Mr. Garrigues) and later still became one of the first women to own and run an advertising agency. But for the rest of her days one ear was never quite right.

May Morrow was only one of thousands of city walkers that afternoon and evening. Nearly all, like May, were obscure people whose little sagas became legends to their families. Perhaps they are still kept alive among their descendants ("And, children, did you ever hear how great-grandpa, in the Blizzard of '88 . . . ?"). Strangely, the walker who was most important in 1888, and about whom the newspapers made a tremendous to-do, is now nearly as forgotten as the beggar child with the basket, even though a life-size statue of him stands upon a pedestal in Madison Square.

Roscoe Conkling was his name. In the 1870s and early 1880s, he had been a senator from New York—*the* man from New York who mattered, a crony of Ulysses S. Grant, and an important figure in the Republican Party. In the national election years of 1876 and 1880, Conkling was often mentioned as a potential candidate for the presidency. Most Republicans thinking of running for office or wanting a government appointment had been careful to stay on his right side. According to one of his most distinguished contemporaries, Elihu Root, "Mr. Conkling was the supreme ruler of this State; the Governor did not count, the legislature did not count; controllers and secretaries of state, and what-not did not count. It was what Mr. Conkling said." Grant, during his presidency, had offered to make Conkling chief justice, to follow Salmon Chase, but he had declined. The job, he said, was too restrictive, and he "would be forever gnawing at the chains."

Chains were perhaps what Conkling needed. He had a poorly controlled temper and made unnecessary enemies because of "the monomania of his own importance"—in the words of President Rutherford B. Hayes, who was one of those unnecessary enemies. He was also highly vindictive and never forgave a grievance, real or fancied.

"Roscoe Conkling was created by nature for a great career. That he missed it was entirely his own fault," Chauncey Depew wrote in his memoirs. "Physically he was the handsomest man of his time. His mental equipment nearly approached genius. His oratorical gifts were of the highest order, and he was a debater of rare power and resources. But his intolerable egotism deprived him of vision necessary for supreme leadership."

Conkling's political downfall had come about in 1881, when Vice-President Hayes succeeded to the presidency (following the assassination of President James A. Garfield). After that, his influence waned. When his term as senator was up, he was not appointed again. He went into private law practice in New York City, where his services were much in demand by the rich and powerful. Jay Gould was among his clients.

Now, in March 1888, he was about to take charge of the defense in the most important civil case of the decade. The widow of the multimillionaire merchant A.T. Stewart had died, her will was being contested, and eighty million dollars were at stake (the equivalent of nearly a billion dollars today). Conkling had not been so excited and engrossed by anything since his days of political power. The case was scheduled to be tried in Superior Court, starting on Monday morning, March 12.

Conkling, a tall, athletic man of fifty-eight, was in the habit of walking downtown every day from his rooms at the Hoffman House, a fashionable hotel on Madison Square. Whether or not he did so that morning is not recorded, but he arrived at Superior Court bright and early. After waiting several hours, he concluded that he was the only lawyer on his side of the courtroom who was going to appear at all. The lawyer in charge of the plaintiffs' legal team, the well-known Joseph Choate, had apparently stayed home. With no plaintiffs, no defendants, and not even a judge, the case was postponed to the next day. Disgusted, Conkling walked across Chambers Street to the Stewart Building, on the corner of Broadway, where he wanted to see some papers. No one was there to show them to him, so he went to his office and worked the rest of the day. He was much too busy to look out of the window, or even to listen to what those few others in the office were saying about the weather.

Soon after five o'clock, a young lawyer named William Sulzer saw Conkling leave the building and offered to find a cab that they might share.

"That depends on the price," Conkling said gruffly.

Sulzer had heard that drivers were asking as much as fifty dollars for a ride as far as Madison Square. Conkling was indignant. "I don't know about you, young man, but I'm strong enough to walk," he said, and started doing so—so fast that Sulzer, who was going the same way, could hardly keep up with him. The wind whirled so much snow and debris in their faces that they could hardly see St. Paul's churchyard as they passed by its iron fence. The tombs might as well have been igloos. The sidewalk was not shoveled, but the snow had been stamped down by enough feet to make a narrow path.

Young Sulzer, a natural politician (he later became governor of New York), had thought to make a useful friendship by sharing the blizzard with this distinguished man, but Conkling was clearly in no mood for chatting. Sulzer, therefore, bid him good night as they came abreast of the Astor House and went inside to secure a room for the night. Instead, he bought the last available sleeping space on a billiard table.

Conkling continued walking. He was not accustomed to giving in to trivial annoyances, such as the weather; and having been raised in upper New York State, he was hard to impress with anything as ordinary as a snowstorm.

"I went magnificently along, shouldering through drifts and headed for the north," he told reporters the next day. Certainly he was in much better shape for a man of nearly sixty than most of his contemporaries, who were fond of nine-course meals and riding about in carriages. Conkling ate moderately, drank very little, and was accustomed to working out daily with bar bells and punching bags. Nevertheless, he told the reporters, "I was pretty well exhausted when I got to Union Square, and wiping the snow from my eyes, tried to make out the triangles there. But it was impossible. There was no light, and I plunged right on in as straight a line as I could. Sometimes I have run across passages in novels of great adventures in snow storms; for example, in stories of Russian life where there would be a vivid description of a man's struggle on a snow-swept and windy plain;

I have always considered them exaggerations, but I shall never say so again. As a matter of fact, the strongest description would fail to approximate the truth."

Usually, when Conkling walked the streets, people recognized him and might come up to ask to shake his hand. But today, nearly all pedestrians were walking with heads down and in the same direction as he. In Union Square, as he stopped for respite, holding on to the base of a gaslight, he noticed a man who was reeling and about to fall, and shouted to him to hang on. The man shared the gaslight stanchion for a minute and peered intently at Conkling.

"Are you—?" he shouted over the wind. "Sir, could you be the great and famous Roscoe Conkling?"

Conkling nodded briefly. Usually he enjoyed an adulatory greeting, but not under these Russian conditions. His admirer held out a snowy glove and told him that they had once been on a jury together. His name, he said, was Rufus Smith, and he had walked from his men's furnishings store downtown at 36 Broad Street.

"You've still got your yellow hair and your big moustache," Smith said. " 'War-God of the Norsemen,' the papers used to call you."

Conkling nodded again, let go of the stanchion, and plowed onward. Not being in politics any more, there was no need to overdo the social niceties.

The two-mile walk to Union Square had taken him two hours. Another hour was consumed in struggling along the Ladies' Mile, and arriving six blocks north at Madison Square. By then his eyebrows and lashes were so caked with ice that he had to stop and try to melt it by holding his hands over his eyes. Even so he could hardly see; the night was too dark and the snow too blinding. Trying to take a shortcut across the square, he soon blundered into a drift up to his armpits.

"For nearly twenty minutes I was stuck there and I came as near giving up and sinking down there to die as a man can and not do it," he told reporters. He did not, however, mention what he had thought about, when a reporter asked if his whole life flashed before him. Had he thought of his triumphs in the Senate, or of how his brilliant sarcasm had demolished his opponents and brought his colleagues cheering to their feet? But the reporter stopped short of asking if he remembered the clapping and genteel hurrahs from the ladies' gallery.

Women had always adored Conkling, and since his wife disliked Washington, much preferring life in small-town upper New York State, he had always been much in demand as an extra man at dinners. In the Senate, the ladies' gallery was likely to be crowded when he was scheduled to speak. During most of the 1870s, one particular lady had often been present, a fact that had not gone unnoticed by the gossips. She was the prominent Washington socialite and beauty, Mrs. Kate Chase Sprague, the daughter of Lincoln's secretary of the treasury and, later, chief justice, Salmon P. Chase, and the wife of William Sprague, governor of Rhode Island during the Civil War, and later senator. "Proud Kate," she had often been called by the press, as well as by people who thought she was far too impressed with herself.

She and Conkling were apparently the only two in Washington who supposed their interest in each other was a secret. Kate's pride was perhaps arrogance, and she felt free to do as she pleased. Sometimes, while seated in the ladies' gallery, she would scribble a note and send it off by one of the black messengers. The next thing anybody knew, the senior senator from New York was standing in front of one of the closed Senate chamber doors with his hands behind his back. Soon the door would open slightly, and a black hand would be observed pressing a bit of paper into Conkling's casually waiting hands.

He would then move away and when (marvel of marvels) he thought no one was looking, he would read the little note and even press it to his lips as he raised his blue eyes toward the ladies' gallery. He was easily as arrogant as his beautiful friend.

It was amazing how indiscreet the two were. Mrs. Sprague had a house in Washington and was often alone there when her husband was detained in Rhode Island. The senator from New York often called, presumably advising the lady about various legal problems that were on her mind. On one occasion, when both were invited to the same dinner party, Conkling was seen waiting by the door with a bunch of red roses. When Mrs. Sprague swept in, he pressed them into her arms. The summer that Mrs. Sprague took a house in Paris turned out to be the very summer that the senator from New York chose to improve, at first hand, his understanding of French politics.

The relationship finally ended when a Providence newspaper reported that Sprague had ejected Senator Conkling from the Spragues' summer home near Narragansett, and had chased him down the road with a shotgun. The Spragues were subsequently divorced, but Conkling remained married to the lady in upper New York State and continued as a busy Washington dinner guest. Kate was less fortunate. Her money dwindled as her beauty faded, and she spent her last years in seclusion, caring for a retarded daughter and selling eggs and chickens from her late father's now dilapidated house outside Washington.

But it was not Conkling's presumed adultery that brought about his political downfall; it was President Hayes's dislike and also what Senator James Blaine (Conkling's most dangerous enemy) referred to on the Senate floor as "his haughty disdain, his grandiloquent swell, his majestic, super-eminent, overpowering turkey-gobbler strut."

If Conkling remembered any of this during his twenty minutes facing death in a snowdrift, he did not talk about it. He managed to struggle out of the drift, "and made my way along. When I reached the New York Club at Twenty-fifth Street I was covered all over with ice and packed snow, and they would scarcely believe me that I had walked from Wall Street."

Conkling collapsed on the doorstep of the club and had to be carried the short way to his hotel. Next day he went downtown again, this time by cab, and talked to the press, but he had a splitting earache, went home as soon as he could, and took to bed. By the weekend, he was extremely ill with mastoiditis and pneumonia.

Among the last walkers to get home that night, and who had the most trying experiences, were those who had put too much faith in els or ferries. Headquarters of the four elevated lines sent notices to be posted at all stations: No Trains Running. But this was not exactly true. A few trains, about one-tenth the usual number, were running—just enough to arouse false hopes of an easy trip home. Before dark, no more tickets were being sold, but the platforms were packed with trusting customers. Some waited up to three hours for trains that, when they did arrive, whizzed right past. The cars were so overloaded that the flanges of the wheels grated against the floors.

Some southbound trains that had stalled that morning were only just beginning to move by late afternoon. At four o'clock, a Sixth Avenue train was backed up a couple of miles to 59th Street and was then sent down Ninth Avenue. Most of the passengers, cooped up since morning, fled to the street, but one dedicated soul, a clerk, stayed aboard and rode down to Chambers Street, where he tried to report for work. His office was closed, but he was lucky enough to find a nearby hotel room for the night.

Perhaps the greatest hardship of any el rider was suffered by Arthur White, a visitor from Long Island who had spent Sunday night with friends at the 57th Street apartment house, the Osborne. Having business downtown on Monday morning, he boarded a Sixth Avenue train and soon found it joining other stalled trains below 14th Street. "Looking out the window we could see train after train on ahead extending in a solid line far beyond the next station. To add to our discomfort the steam went down in the engine, and the cars grew colder and colder." As lunchtime approached, someone lowered a basket full of cash to the street. Boys on the street—honest ones—filled the basket with sandwiches from a nearby restaurant. After six miserable hours had passed, firemen came with ladders and helped everyone to descend.

Mr. White, still with his mind on business, made for the Third Avenue el, but found no trains running downtown. He then decided to go home to Long Island. An el took him north to 34th Street, and he then walked two blocks east "in raging wind and stinging frozen snow" and took a ferry to Long Island City—only to find the train terminal there packed with weary commuters, all sitting or lying on the floor. No trains were running, or likely to run, on the Long Island Railroad.

White, a hard man to discourage, then recrossed the East River, got another el to 59th Street, and walked west to seek shelter with his friends at the Osborne. "More than once a sleepy feeling would creep over me, and I thought it would be Heaven if I could lie down in the snow and take a nap. Hardly a soul was on the streets (it was now late in the evening) and a deathly silence prevailed over the usually busy, noisy city." But he did arrive at the Osborne—and lived many more years.

Charles Macdonald, who lived on 128th Street near Eighth Avenue, walked miles that morning in order to reach his downtown office. At three o'clock he started homeward in company with a friend who "had been a woodsman and trapper and scoffed at the idea of not getting home easily." After trying all four el lines, they finally managed to board a northbound Second Avenue train. They arrived at 125th Street "and began to walk west through snow banks facing a high wind that blew clouds of snow in our faces. As we passed over the bridge at Park Avenue we noticed that the depot . . . was completely covered by snow." The railroad tracks, which were then below ground level, were snowed in to the level of the street. Drifts of snow against houses on 125th Street were two stories high in some places. "We made several stops at shops on the way, drinking hot tea and coffee. I also had a supply of chocolate which we ate. . . . My companion [the woodsman and trapper] was 'all in' at the finish. Not so easy after all!"

William T. Rehm, an optician, lived in the Bronx but got himself downtown Monday morning just in time for lunch. At 1:30, "I turned my back on business and started for home." The reason for his haste was that he was going to a masquerade ball that evening, "one of the town's social events," where he was to play the part of Prince Carnival. From Fulton Street, he walked most of the way to 150th Street in the Bronx, a distance of about nine miles, stopping off for an occasional ale with lots of red pepper. ("The drink gave me considerable inward warmth.") At 110th Street, he began to worry about crossing the Harlem River, for the wind and sleet were very sharp. Happily, an elevated shuttle train was running, and he rode part of the way. "Of course, I made the Masquerade Ball, but it was all in vain. It had to be postponed. Only a few men attended and one woman. She had to be carried on the back of her escort."

As for the ferries, those to Staten Island gave up in the early afternoon. "The wind snapped off the flagstaffs of the *Northfield* and *Westfield*," reported the *Sun*, "the instant they left their piers in the morning. . . . Where the wind had full play from the northwest, the boats skimmed along like a lightning express, but the helms were practically useless, because the boats wouldn't answer them. The Captains had to trust to luck to reach their piers. Captain Cattermale, who has been twenty years in the service of the ferry company, said that in all his life he never knew the wind to blow over the waters with such furious vigor."

Ferries on the two rivers continued to ply, with varying degrees of success. "Only a few persons ventured out of the cabins, and those whom curiosity led to do so were nearly thrown flat upon the deck by the blast." There was more and more ice coming down the Hudson and, when the tide turned, backing up the East River in huge chunks. One of the Chambers Street ferries got caught in heavy ice as it tried to enter its slip and had to wait two hours for a tug to pull it around. Passengers crowded all the ferry stations, and many spent the night in them.

"Nothing could describe the fury of the wind or the black desolation of the scene out on the North [Hudson] River," wrote a *Sun* reporter. "The snow, driven by the wind, made an impenetrable veil, which the sharpest eye could not pierce more than 200 feet from the boat. Here and there, as the wind lulled or shifted for an instant, another ferryboat might be seen, looming spectre-like and alarmingly near at hand."

Those who could find no transportation and preferred not to walk took refuge in bars if they had a little money. New York City had an average of six saloons or liquor stores to the block, so it was not hard to find one. But there is considerable danger in drinking a lot and then going out into a blizzard. A number of those found dead in the snow had heavy fumes of alcohol about them. One homeward-bound walker, George Pitman, on his way through the Broadway district, saw a man stagger from a saloon and dive headfirst into a snowbank, leaving only his legs waving in the air. Pitman dragged him back inside, probably saving his life.

Despite its hazards, whiskey was the popular restorative. A driver attempting to deliver a boiler in a four-horse dray bought a quart of whiskey and poured it equally down the throats of his animals. The boiler was delivered.

A horse pulling a hearse was rescued from a drift by some of the New York *World* staff, who must have had a drop of whiskey themselves. They unhitched the animal and took him up a flight of stairs to the newsroom. His life was saved, but next day they had to use a block and tackle to get him out.

William O'Connor, a young broker who lived on East 12th Street, spent Monday morning getting to Grand Central to meet his sister. Finding the station without trains or any prospect of any, he set out for home, walking down Fifth Avenue. At 37th Street, he came upon a stage, stuck in the snow although it was drawn by four sturdy horses. (A stage cost twice as much—twenty cents—as the horsecar because it had no standing room. It was an ancestor of Fifth Avenue's double-decker motor buses, which also had no standing room.) The driver sat on the box, almost frozen to the seat, and unable to handle the reins with his frostbitten hands. O'Connor helped him unhitch the horses and took him into the nearby St. Nicholas Club, of which he was a member. Plied with apple-whiskey toddies, the driver was revived to a point where he was able to mount one of the horses and lead them all to their stable. O'Connor then proceeded home by way of four more bars.

8

Helping

"NEW YORKERS," wrote the New York *Times*, "are the best-natured people in the world."

There was much good humor shown through all the blizzard's discomforts and dangers, and much genuine kindness toward strangers and chivalry toward women. Fifty years later, when old-timers recalled the Blizzard of '88, this was a recurrent theme: "Those were the happy days!" one of the "Blizzard Men" said. "No war, no enemies, and no race prejudice—everyone was a good neighbor and democratic."

But how well had the Blizzard Man remembered? It is true that the exigencies of the storm prompted the setting aside of some of the standard prejudices of class, race, and sex, but those prejudices remained, nonetheless. Italians, Irish, Germans, Jews, among countless other groups engaged in the scramble for a better life, often got in one another's way, while the dominant Anglo-Saxons were likely to frown upon them all. Blacks were the lowest on this totem pole, and they are so seldom mentioned in the annals of the blizzard that one wonders if they were invisible. One blizzard veteran remembered being pulled from a drift by "a young colored chap," and blacks manned some of the ladders by which people escaped from stalled el trains. But how many there were, or what they did for a living, is nowhere recorded. People criticized them for charging too much for the ladder service, but whether it was ten cents, twenty-five, or fifty was not recorded either. Blacks turned up to carry bags, fetch sandwiches, run after blown-away hats—and quickly disappeared again. The *World* spoke of the "colored squatters" who lived in Hackensack Meadows. Late Monday night their bonfires could be seen, burning in the huge expanse of snow. But how they lived, how they ate and kept warm, how they felt about anything, or what their names were—all that is gone with the ashes of the bonfires.

Yet good nature, helpfulness, and sometimes true heroism were in marked evidence. A janitor, headed for work downtown, helped a frail woman schoolteacher to the el platform: "The wind nearly carried both of us away." A Macy's floor-walker, John Schneider, noticed an old woman cowering in a 14th Street vestibule. He spoke to her, and learned that she had been put out of her furnished room that morning for nonpayment of rent. Schneider risked being late for work and took her to a home for the indigent. And a young dry-goods clerk carried a fellow worker, who had become ill and was unable to walk, all the way from Fulton Street to the ferry station at the Battery. It took him three hours, carrying the man piggyback along the slippery sidewalks. Still another young man found a bewildered shopgirl wandering disoriented on Bleecker Street, and escorted her to her home, some eighty-five blocks away. Her mother, when they arrived about midnight, fainted with joy and the girl "smothered him with kisses."

The master of a cotton schooner from Savannah had seen the barometer dropping and hurried to make port at the South Street docks. In front of a nearby saloon, he found a woman nearly unconscious. Rather than take her into the saloon, which was filled with sailors, he carried her to his schooner, where he and the mate revived her with coffee. She was exhausted. "When you are ready, Miss, just retire to my room and lock the door," said the chivalrous Georgian. And she did.

A truck driver for the American Express Company, John Henry Hard, had the most trying day of his life. While he was making his first stop on Canal Street, falling wires blew on top of his team and truck. The police spent an hour getting the wires off and untangled. Hard then kept at his deliveries for several more painful hours until his boss sent a messenger to tell him to go back to the stable. Although his hands, face, and ears were frostbitten and he badly needed food, he stopped to give a lift to a bevy of twelve homeward-bound factory girls. He packed them into the wagon and let them borrow the blankets with which he protected his merchandise. The girls got home, Hard survived, and the horses made it to the stable, although they fell from exhaustion as they tried to go up the run into the barn.

Charles Hentz worked at Castle Garden, where thirty-five hundred immigrants were waiting to be processed and take trains for the West. They were allowed to spend two nights sleeping on the floors and benches, and not until Wednesday could they be sent on their way. Meantime, they had to be fed. Hentz volunteered to go to 18th Street to get some meat that had been ordered but had not arrived. He went on foot, hoping to return with the meat in the butcher's wagon, but found the butcher shop closed. Starting back downtown, he was set upon by thugs on Greenwich Street, robbed, and thrown headfirst into a drift. A policeman saved him and walked with him to a safe neighborhood, saying that a man had been killed on that very spot earlier in the day.

Like the God of the Old Testament, the police of New York City could be terrible in vengeance but helpful to the righteous. To the upper and working classes, the cop on the beat was a pleasant, polite fellow, most likely Irish, sauntering along, twirling a billy club, and giving honest citizens a sense of security. He patted children on the head and winked at the nurse or mother as he stopped traffic for her and the baby carriage. Sometimes the servants in the big brownstones invited him in for coffee and pie, and householders gave him a little cash present at Christmastime. But for the very poor, for blacks, and for new immigrants from Europe who did not speak English, he was likely to seem a frightening bully. Street urchins and peddlers scurried away when he approached, and anyone arrested for a real or suspected offense was likely to find out what a policeman's club was for. In 1888, the police inspector who oversaw the poorest and most dangerous parts of the lower East Side was one Alexander Williams, known to friends and enemies alike as "Clubber" Williams. He was once quoted as saying, "There is more law in a night stick than in all the statute books."

"Clubber" himself had been in court often. By 1888, 358 complaints, mostly for brutality, had been lodged against him, and he had paid 224 fines. Nevertheless, he was a powerful figure. Although his salary was modest, he owned a house on East 10th Street, an estate at Cos Cob, Connecticut, and a steam yacht. The funds he needed to keep up these amenities came from selling "protection" to gambling halls on the Bowery and houses of prostitution in the Tenderloin district. Mayor Hewitt, in carrying out his drive to close the worst of the city's brothels and dives, ignored a target list suggested to him by Williams and instead hired a private detective to compile a more objective one.

Two years later, Congress held an investigation of the New York City Police Department. Besides looking into allegations of brutality and corruption, attention was given to such police irregularities as imprisonment without cause, extortion, violation of excise laws, tampering with ballot boxes, and intimidation of Republicans. Nonetheless, New York's Finest* included many honest and conscientious men. Their hours were long, their pay low, and their jobs dangerous. On the lower East Side, the population was very dense, sometimes comprising as many as a thousand people an acre, far more than in comparable parts of London. In the whole world, only the slums of Bombay were as crowded. And New York slums were difficult to police, in view of their polyglot denizens.

In addition to trying to keep order and apprehend criminals, the New York City police also had to deal with the homeless. At that time (and until 1896) the only shelters in the city aside from the few offered by private charities were the station houses, where the homeless were allowed to spend the night sleeping on bare benches or on the floor—men, women, and children alike. One private shelter was known as the Home for Friendless and Fallen Women; all other private shelters for women admitted only those who had not fallen—although it must have been hard to tell, by looking at a woebegone face, whether its owner might not be a hussy masquerading as a good girl until the weather got nicer. Anyone suspected of such deception was left standing in the snow, in order to protect the morals of those inside. As a last resort, a woman might try to be arrested for some misdemeanor in order to be thrown into a jail cell. But jail

*The phrase was coined by Mayor William F. Havemeyer in 1874.

cells could be dangerous, for they were shared by both sexes and by the insane. Only that year had the state legislature passed a bill authorizing (but not requiring) separate cells for female prisoners, and the use of matrons to guard them, rather than policemen.

Homeless children fared slightly better than adults. Since 1853 New York had had a newsboys' shelter, and there were asylums for orphans and for homeless or deserted minors. For abandoned babies there was the New York Foundling Asylum, which had begun to receive them in the early 1870s, despite a general public opinion that caring for unwanted infants would only encourage women to have more. By 1888, an average of twenty babies a week were turning up in the nuns' doorstep basket; but during the week of the blizzard there were only seven.

Three police stations in the city had telephones, and the other thirty-two had to make do with telegrams and messengers. A patrolman in need of help had no way of calling for it. All police communication failed during the blizzard, except for messengers, who were rookie policemen; some of them made heroic walks of a hundred blocks or more. Each precinct had two platoons; one was out on patrol while the other stayed on reserve in the station house. The men all worked sixteen hours a day. In addition, they were frequently recalled to the station house and ordered to court duty or to control strikes, riots, or parades. During the blizzard police hours were not even tallied, and the force performed difficult tasks of all kinds, some gruesome, others outlandish.

Patrolman Daniel Quigley, of Brooklyn, was just finishing up his station-house duty on Sunday evening, March 11, when a drunk came in and asked the desk sergeant to lock him up. He needed sleep, he said, even though he knew it meant going to court the next day and facing a penalty for drunkenness. The sergeant obliged and put Quigley's name down as the officer who would take the prisoner to court.

At midnight, Quigley went on duty with his platoon to a post in Greenpoint, known as Dangertown. He spent the night on the streets, encountering no trouble from the criminal element but a great deal in the way of rain, sleet, wind, and snow. At 6 A.M. he returned to the station, wet and cold, and at eight, woke his prisoner. As no horsecars or any other vehicles were running, the two of them walked three miles through knee-deep snow to the court on Bushwick Avenue. Quigley told the judge that the prisoner had been "very agreeable during our disagreeable walk," and the judge discharged him, well sobered up and badly hung over. Quigley then walked three more miles to his home, had dinner, and returned—three more miles—to the station, ready for patrol. He did not go off duty until midnight, having worked steadily for twenty-four hours and having walked, including his post duty, a total of seventeen miles.

More than one blizzard victim was hauled from a snowdrift, more dead than alive, by a policeman. And many who walked the streets during those days remembered seeing policemen rubbing people's ears with snow (heroically if misguidedly) in order to prevent frostbite. The New York *Times* noted, "In almost every hallway a policeman had a patient, whose ears he vigorously rubbed."

In 1888, doctors not only made house calls, but made them—or tried to—during blizzards. Every village, town, and city in the Northeast could tell stories of heroic doctors who struggled through drifts and across fields in buggies and sleighs, on snowshoes and on foot. Most emergency calls were for childbirth, and many babies were born during the blizzard without the help of doctors—but not because the doctors were lounging cozily at home.

A medical man named Nascher had a patient on the upper East Side whose baby was due any minute. Since he had assured the prospective parents that he would be there when the time came, on Monday morning he took his bag and walked nearly five miles, from Greenwich Village to East 87th Street. When he arrived, after what seemed at the time to have been the most terrible experience of his life, his patient's husband met him at the door. Where the devil had he been? The baby had already been born—no thanks to him. He never wanted to see Dr. Nascher again or any other such irresponsible person, and neither did his wife. "Get out of my house!" he finished, and sent the unfortunate doctor back into the storm. Nascher tied his bag onto his back with bandages, and went slogging off. His return trip was even worse; it took him seven hours to get home.

Andrew J. Fox was interning at the state hospital on Ward's Island in the East River. On Sunday evening he returned by rowboat from family visits in Manhattan—a perilous trip, in view of ice floes and the strong wind—landing across from 116th Street and then walking the equivalent of twenty-six blocks to visit his wards. Returning to the interns' quarters, he was told that "it was almost impossible to exist outside," let alone visit the wards. But next day, he and another young doctor set out to do just that. They rescued a Lutheran minister, who was "struggling exhausted in a drift," visited their patients, checked others in the Quarantine Building, and then trudged back to their quarters, "a most exhausting trip." Meanwhile, ice had totally clogged the river and the island was cut off for three days.

Dr. Clarence Smith was an intern at Bellevue. On Monday there was a strange absence of emergencies, because the telegraph and telephone were out of commission and because the one-horse ambulances could not get through the streets. But after about twenty-four hours, when emergency cases came or were carried in, there were more admissions than ever. Broken bones, pneumonia, frostbite, and ear infections were the chief complaints, and these cases remained abnormally frequent for months after the blizzard; 1888 was a record year for mortality.

Since most people did not have a telephone and could not afford telegrams, children were often used to deliver messages, as they had been since time immemorial. Much more than now, children were sent to the store or on various errands. During the blizzard, many were sent out as usual by parents who had no idea of the storm's ferocity or the danger of the drifts, which were crusted on top but might easily give way and swallow up a small child.

A thirteen-year-old who lived in one of the burgeoning residential areas of upper Manhattan was dispatched on a familiar mission: to buy a day's supply of coal and bring it home in a pail. The new block of flats where he lived stood alone in rocky, hilly terrain otherwise occupied only by squatters' hovels and empty lots. He fell down among drifts and loose boulders in a thirty-five-foot-high cut. Luckily, someone was watching from a window and sent help with rope and shovel.

Little orphan Amy Smith was living with guardians on Beekman Place. The child went out to get milk, wearing a knitted hood and carrying a milk pail. With a toy shovel she made a path down the stoop. At the corner (as she wrote fifty years later, when she became a Blizzard Lady), the wind "which was blowing a gale caught me up, carried me some distance and deposited me in a mountainous snowdrift." A milkman in his wagon and a boy carrying groceries saw "me flying through space but because of drifting snow could not see where I had been buried . . . I was completely lost to sight." They rescued her, and the milkman "sat me in front of him on his huge dray horse (which he had unharnessed) and so I rode to the house with the empty milk pail hanging on my arm."

Father Daniel Cunnion, a priest at the Church of St. Raphael, on West 40th Street, was on his way to visit a sick parishioner when he "heard a wail as of a cat in distress, but on looking about, I spied a little hand just above the snow about half way down the block. I plowed through the snow and picked up a boy of about ten or eleven, recognizing him as one of my Sunday-school children. I picked him up, also his pail of coal, and took him to the top floor of the house where he lived. The mother not sensing, of course, the violence of the storm, had sent the boy across the street to Buttermilk John's store. I do believe that had not Providence guided that boy, he would have died, for the storm was raging more and more." That same evening, his brother, Reverend Malick Cunnion, said "a well-dressed man had been found in the gutter in front of the Rectory of St. Michael's, Ninth Avenue and 31st. He was dead."

Working children were among the heroes of the blizzard. They stuck to their jobs even more tenaciously than most adults, not only because they were young and strong, but also because the money they earned was badly needed at home. Thirteen was the legal age for working, but thousands of younger children had full-time jobs, such as stripping tobacco, making artificial flowers, cutting feathers from cocks' tails (called "stripping feathers"), or performing the simpler tasks of needlework and tailoring. In shops, cash girls and boys were usually twelve or thirteen and made $1.50 or $2 a week. Slightly older girls could make about twice as much, standing behind counters for eleven hours a day, while boys of that age did more rugged work that took them out in the streets.

A butcher boy, Alex Canter, spent Monday delivering meat on foot. All his fingers were frozen and gave him trouble for the rest of his life. A youngster named Frank Stanley arrived at his job at a large downtown importing house after a two-hour walk. He was the only employee there. At eleven, his boss got through to him by telephone, ordering Frank to get the mail from the post office and bring it to him at his home on West 56th Street. Frank ingeniously wrapped his head and face with yards of imported French veiling, cut from a bolt in the stock room, fought his way downtown to the post office, and then uptown to 56th Street. He arrived at 8:30 in the evening, after a five-hour trip on foot. "What kept you so long?" his boss snarled.

Fourteen-year-old Francis J. Hoffman, the oldest of five children, was a cashboy at Lord and Taylor. He made two dollars a week, working weekdays from 8 to 6:30 and Saturdays until 11 P.M. Although the windy snow was "like pieces of sharp broken glass," he had to get there—"I was afraid I would lose my job." He lived only eight blocks from the store, but walking them took an hour. He was a few minutes late, and asked the timekeeper if he would be fined. "Not sure," replied the timekeeper. All employees who made under six dollars a week were customarily fined ten cents if they were five minutes late. If they were later than that, they had to get a pass from the superintendent, or be told to come the next day, forfeiting that day's pay. There were no customers, and Lord and Taylor closed its doors at 11 that morning. Francis found the trip home, facing the wind, even harder. When he got home, crying with pain, his mother rubbed him with home-rendered lard. As it turned out, the superintendent gave all absentees full wages that week. Francis got no extra for coming, but was promoted to be the superintendent's office boy.

Among the bravest were the Western Union boys and the newspaper copy-runners. C. V. La Fumee was a copy-runner at the Brooklyn *Eagle*. His job was to go where reporters had been assigned—courts, police stations, important meetings, and so on—and bring their copy back to the editor. He was out every day of the blizzard, and the *Eagle* rewarded him for "loyalty under hazardous conditions." Another energetic messenger boy from Brooklyn worked all day Monday, much harder than usual, and earned seven dollars in extra pay, the equivalent of three or four weeks' salary.

Western Union boys ranged in age from twelve to fourteen or fifteen. To send a telegram, people contacted the nearest office by pulling a lever (installed by the company in private houses, free of charge), and a boy would appear at the door. Through the days of the blizzard, these boys kept on appearing. It was the telegraph wires, not the boys, that failed. One unfortunate youngster in New Haven, who fought the drifts for several hours before giving up and going home, was fired next day for nonperformance of duty. Western Union was a harsh taskmaster, but it did reward those who kept going with small salary raises.

But the most industrious and enterprising child of all was surely Milton Daub, a twelve-year-old who lived on East 145th Street in the south Bronx. That part of the city was then a pleasant place of farms, estates, and small houses set well back from the street with gardens in front of them. The Daub family—mother, father, and four children—lived in one of these.

On the morning of Monday, March 12, Milton was up early, as usual, getting ready to go to school. Even at 7:30, both front and back doors and windows were already blocked with snow, and Mrs. Daub had the lamps lit. It was soon decided that none of the children should go to school. There was enough food in the house for a day or two, except for milk.

Milton volunteered to go and buy some. "You'll never get to the store," his father said. But Milton's class at school had been studying Eskimos, and based on what he'd just learned about snowshoes, Milton forthwith devised a pair. He used two wooden barrel hoops, wire, twine, pieces of canvas, and roller skates without the wheels.

His father nailed a box top to a sledge, converting it into a sort of express wagon on runners, and put it out the window. Then he tied a clothesline to Milton, who went out the window, too, and took some practice runs on the snowshoes. They seemed to work well, so after wrapping him up warmly, Mr. and Mrs. Daub sent him off to Ash's grocery, with fifty cents in his pocket.

As he skimmed along the snowy street, neighbors called to him from their windows to bring them some milk. When he got to the store he bought fifty cents' worth of condensed milk—the milkman had not been there—but instead of taking it home, he sold it. Although he did not charge more than it cost, he got tips, and in twenty minutes had acquired two dollars. With this he bought a case of condensed milk, sold it, took in tips, bought another case, and so on, all morning. When he heard the noon whistle he went home, taking three cans of milk he had saved for the family.

Scoldings quickly changed to startled praise when Milton showed his parents his pocketsful of coins and bills. After lunch he went out again, wearing three pairs of knitted wool stockings, as his feet were getting a little cold. By three he had sold all the milk that Mr. Ash had in his store. He then switched to another grocery and continued his deliveries. About four o'clock, a woman called to him from a window and asked him to fill a prescription for her sick husband. Milton took the prescription to the druggist and, while waiting for it to be filled, sold another case of milk. "Anyone who comes out in such weather doesn't have to pay for medicine," the druggist said. Milton delivered the prescription, receiving a large tip, and then another lady in the same house gave him a grocery order to fill, with money to pay for it. While that order was being filled, he sold still more milk, and when he delivered the groceries the lady told him to keep all the change.

By that time, he recalled, "it was five o'clock, and I was getting tired. I would have helped others, but I knew I had to be home on time, as my father was very strict."

On the way home he bought bread for the family. "I felt very proud. This is the first time in my young life that I am paying for bread, with money that I had earned for my family."

As he came trudging through the Daubs' front garden, he saw the whole family at the window.

"You surely look tired," said his father, helping him off with the snowshoes.

"Yes, Sir," said Milton.

He gave his mother all the money, ate a hot supper, went to bed, and slept twelve hours.

In the morning, his mother asked him if he had any idea how much he had made. No, he said, but he did know that the tips came to more than the cost of the milk.

"You made $67.65,"* his mother said, "not counting the ten cents you spent for our bread."

On Tuesday, Milton came home from school and shoveled snow.

On Wednesday, he financed a sleigh ride for the family.

---

*The equivalent of about $800 in the money of a hundred years later.

9

After Dark

LATE IN THE AFTERNOON, a wild bird flew into a saloon near Madison Square and stood on the bar for ten minutes. The bartender offered it a drink, which it declined, preferring to stand and stare at the other storm refugees, who were standing and staring at it. Freezing, miserable humanity, wild and tame, also sought shelter in saloons, which were crowded and uproarious all week long. The bird had chosen one of the better ones, but throughout the city, from the Astor House to the dives on the Bowery, bars offered comfort and camaraderie. They also offered free lunches, until supplies ran out. In most saloons, but surely not in the better sort, everyone used the same fork and wiped his mouth on a towel clamped to the bar.

Most all-night bar patrons would probably have preferred a hotel room, but they were hard to come by. Before dark on Monday, hotels had rented almost every room and were going on to rent chairs, closets and, as mentioned before, space on billiard tables. A young man named Chadbourne, who had been walking with a friend all day from a stalled train in upper Manhattan, and had nearly been killed when a fence blew down on top of them, headed for a hotel at Broadway and 38th Street. Chadbourne was a good friend of the manager, Mr. Brue.

Chadbourne and his companion staggered into the lobby about four o'clock, and spotted Brue standing behind the desk.

"For Heaven's sake, Brue," Chadbourne called out, "give us a couple of rooms and a bath."

"I am very sorry, Sir," Brue replied, "but there is not a vacant bed in the house. All I can offer you is a couple of chairs in the office here."

As Chadbourne recalled, "Thereupon I pulled off my hat, and said, 'It is pretty darn tough, Brue, when you cannot find a place for an old friend.' He looked at me a second time and said, 'My God! It's Chadbourne! Look in the mirror if you want to see a sight!'

"I knew my partner looked terribly, his moustache was a wabbly cake of ice which had pounded on his chin as he walked until his chin was bleeding. My face was scratched, red as a lobster, my eyebrows were frozen and my chin was resting on a cake of snowy ice packed in between the top of my overcoat and my bandanna handkerchief. Mr. Brue, God bless him, said, 'You and your friend go down to the washroom and get your coats, shoes and socks off and I will try and find a place for you.'

"By the time we got our coats and outside woolen hose off and got the snow and ice brushed off our clothing, Mr. Brue came down and told us to come up to his apartment. He had had a bed put up in his own parlor where an open fire was burning briskly. Fortunately for us a gentleman's furnishings store was in the same building as the hotel and this was open so we were able to purchase fresh underwear, and after a good rub-down we jumped into bed and took a nap and got up about six o'clock, dressed in fresh linen and with our clothes dried out and pressed we arrived downstairs feeling like a couple of young fighting cocks."

They stayed at the hotel for three days, patronizing the restaurant and bar. The train they had left on Monday morning arrived at Grand Central on Thursday, bringing their luggage; and on Friday the two went to Philadelphia, their destination in the first place.

Even those who could afford expensive suites wound up on cots in hotel lobbies. Suites were turned into dormitories, and blankets and sheets were shared by strangers. In a few hours, even the most modern, fastidiously run hotels regressed to the level of medieval wayside inns. When the Hanover Bank asked for accomodations for fifteen employees, all fifteen were put in one room. The Astor House turned away more than a thousand applicants. And an elderly lady, a frequent Astor patron, was lucky to get a bathroom, with a bed made up in the tub. One man who arrived in the late evening at a hotel near the Brooklyn Bridge, having reserved and paid for a room that morning, found only a bedstead with three slats. Other patrons had managed to pick the lock and had borrowed all the bed-clothes, the mattress, the springs, and one of the slats.

A little boy named Charlie, from Cape Cod, had arrived in New York on Sunday with his father, a shoe-factory owner, and they lodged at the Gilsey House, at Broadway and 29th Street. His father had come to buy shoe leather, and had promised Charlie a trip to the circus. But all Charlie ever saw of either the circus or the city was a view of Broadway, with snow-drifts halfway up to the hotel dining-room windows. "Everybody in the hotel was marooned," he reminisced. "There was a big business in 'toddies.' I didn't know exactly what they were at the time, but Father and his friends certainly punished a bunch."

———

Had Charlie's father not spent so much time on toddies, he might have taken his son to the Barnum and Bailey Circus, only four blocks away. It was scheduled to open on Monday afternoon, and it did. James Bailey got there by Sixth Avenue el early in the morning, all the way from his home near West 150th Street; and Barnum came by carriage from the Murray Hill Hotel. That was a journey of only fourteen blocks, but his public felt sure he would have got there no matter how far he had had to come. He never missed an opening, and always rode into the arena in his carriage, smiling and leaning down to shake hands with the children and ask if they were having a good time. He was as much a part of the circus as the clowns and trained elephants. That day he stood up in his carriage and said to the audience (which, in an arena that would hold twelve thousand, numbered a scanty hundred), "The storm may be a great show, but I still have the greatest show on earth!"

At both afternoon and evening performances, all through the week, every one of the eighty-six acts in three rings went on as scheduled, while the constant din of the band drowned out the scraping of more than a hundred shovels on the flat roof of Madison Square Garden.

The Garden, as it has always been called by New Yorkers, was then nearing the end of its first incarnation. The unprepossessing building it occupied, at the northeast corner of Madison Square, was a former train shed and stable belonging to the New York and Harlem Railroad. From the 1840s to the 1870s, steam locomotives were not allowed in the city below 32nd Street, and for that reason, the railroad had kept horses there to draw its trains up Fourth Avenue to the point where locomotives could take over. After the law was repealed, Barnum bought the place, turned it into a "Great Roman Hippodrome"

270 feet long, and rented it out for revival meetings, flower shows, and the first Westminster Kennel Club Show (1877). Later, others used it for riding shows, ice carnivals, and boxing; and in 1879 William H. Vanderbilt and a syndicate bought and redecorated it, and named it Madison Square Garden. The place remained a popular spot for all sorts of exhibitions that needed plenty of space until 1889, when the owners would tear it down and replace it with a far more imposing edifice, designed by McKim, Mead and White.

Reviewing the circus, the *Sun* remarked, "To a philosopher like Phineas Taylor Barnum, whose big show has wrestled with six fires and come out of them greater than ever, a thing like the blizzard was simply a new form of experience."

Most theaters, however, were dark that Monday evening: their losses were later estimated at a total of twenty thousand dollars. Only three Broadway shows gave performances. Broadway, below the present Times Square, was where the best and newest theaters were, many built during the 1880s to replace others that had burned down—for theaters, with their open gas-flames and combustible curtains and scenery, burned down frequently. At one of the city's older theaters, on 13th Street, Henry Irving and Ellen Terry, playing in *Faust*, managed to get there by carriage, and Miss Terry was carried inside by admirers, but the audience was sparse. We do not know whether or not Mark Twain attended, but one suspects that he remained despondent in his room at the Murray Hill Hotel. His wife did not join him from Hartford until three days later.

At the old Academy of Music, on 14th Street and Irving Place, the noted German tragedian Ludwig Barnay was to appear in *Kean* (a play by Dumas père about the noted English tragedian). Herr Barnay and all the other actors were brought from their lodgings in cabs at fifteen dollars apiece, but with only eight customers in the orchestra and not more than a hundred in the galleries at curtain time, a postponement was announced. "Many of those who had braved the storm were keenly grieved," said the *Sun*, "and expressed their feelings roundly."

But another 14th Street theater, Tony Pastor's, which specialized in musical variety shows, opened its doors as usual and provided a performance to a sea of empty seats. Francis J. Pfister, who was spending the night at his bookbindery in the next block and was in the balcony with two of his employees, described the evening: "The audience consisted of just four persons, including the three of us and one other man. When it came time for the show to start, Mr. Pastor came to the footlights and said owing to the weather only a few of his performers had shown up and a few musicians. He said if he wished we could go to the box office and get a refund; he announced the total receipts were a dollar; however, that did not matter, if we wished he would go on with the show with what he had. I called down to go on with the show. The orchestra consisted of five men, and the performers were Maggie Cline [in street clothes, as her costume trunks had not arrived] and a husband and wife duo styled as the Reed Birds. All the performers responded to our applause just the same as if the house was crowded." After the show, Mr. Pfister and his two companions went back to the bindery and had a fine sleep, on piles of shavings.

TUESDAY, MARCH 13

Tuesday,
March 13

O N TUESDAY the Boston *Transcript* finally turned its attention to the storm. It was hard to rattle this staid newspaper, but it did put the blizzard story in headlines: BOSTON LITERALLY SNOWED IN. Its weather writer favored a somewhat literary style for his forecasts. Where someone else might have written "cloudy and colder," his Saturday copy had predicted "a sky veiled in gray, vanes pointing eastward, a rawness in the air." For Tuesday, March 13, he spoke of torrents of rain and soft, rainy snow, "an icy porridge."

The *Transcript* went on to say that Boston and New York ("the two chief cities of the country") were cut off from each other, and "pedestrianism this morning was out of the question for those who sought to make progress."

Philadelphia was much harder hit than Boston, but its leading newspaper, the *Bulletin*, also refused to be stampeded into sensationalism. A story on page six of the Tuesday edition spoke of "the most disagreeable snow storm of the season," and told of stalled trains and horsecars and difficulties in getting to

135

work. One reporter, with not much solid news to write about (and perhaps reluctant to go out looking for any), soared to flights of fancy: "The long stretches of electric and telegraph lines were turned into aeolian harps by the winds, and nocturnes and Wagnerian symphonies were rattled off at a lively rate, the poles to which the wires were attached frantically swaying to and fro as if trying to beat time for the wild harmonies." And "the back gate would have to be advertised for—there was no back yard. It had been lost, strayed or stolen and a marble quarry left to fill its place."

For Springfield and New Haven newspapers, both in the hardest-hit area, the greatest interest lay in stranded travelers. At Springfield, the hotels were overflowing, and at the stations all available Pullman berths were in use. Withal, there was gaiety—singing, dancing, and cards—and at the Massesoit House an Irish song-and-dance team, Murray and Murphy, obligingly kept doing their act. Mingling together were "all sorts," reported the Springfield *Republican*, "the slightly suspicious New Yorker, the jovial, hospitable-smiled merchant from the Far West." Also among the stranded was the eminent New Orleans writer, George Washington Cable.

In New Haven, the vice-president of the New York, New Haven and Hartford said that even five thousand shovelers couldn't get a train out of there on Tuesday. Aboard the Hartford–Florida express, stalled on the outskirts of New Haven for fifty-six hours, was a Brooklyn businessman, Charles Parsons, with his pretty daughter, described as "a society belle." The New Haven *Register* reported, "When the shades of evening had fallen a quartet of Yalensians risked bodily injury in seeking out the stalled train, and seranaded the inmates, Miss Parsons, of course, being the magnetic center of attraction."

At Newport, the breakers were said to be "the largest ever seen," and the chief of the lifesaving station was quoted as saying that the sea was the worst he had ever experienced. Block Island was stormbound.

Before dawn in New York City, snow ceased to fall for a while, but the cold was intense, the temperature nearly zero, and the wind was still gusting high. At about 2 A.M., a supervisor for the Metropolitan Telephone and Telegraph Company, William Eckert, was making his way along a downtown street enroute to his Cortlandt Street office, where he would meet repairmen and discuss what had to be done. He was trying to hurry and keep his footing at the same time, when he heard the sound of sobbing, coming from an entranceway. He turned back and peered into the dark corners, and there, huddled together on a doormat, were two little girls. They wore only shawls over thin dresses, and were clinging to one another, shaking with cold. Eckert picked them up, one over each shoulder, and carried them to his office. The repairmen shared hot coffee and sandwiches with them and rubbed their ears and hands.

When the children were sufficiently revived, they said their names were Rosa and Lucia, aged eleven and twelve, and that they were tobacco strippers and worked in Jersey City. They had started home as usual, at seven on Monday evening, but the ferry had been detained by ice. Then, when they were walking from the ferry landing after midnight, the streets had looked so strange and different in the snow that they had lost their way. Eckert assigned two of his repairmen to take them to their home on Cherry Street and to their frantic mother.

"Stay home tomorrow," he advised them kindly. "It's no weather for little girls. But if you have big brothers, send them to my office. Tell them we'll pay better for shoveling than the railroad or anyone else."

Hiring shovelers and hanging on to them had become, in twenty-four hours, a cutthroat affair. Immigrants who arrived that week were snapped up before they had gone more than a block or two from Castle Garden. "The man with the shovel is our representative Italian today," someone wrote. Often as many as fifteen thousand Italians a day came off the ships from Naples, most of them with no more than ten dollars in their pockets and pathetically vulnerable to the unscrupulous recruiters who met each ship and talked the unwary immigrants into signing up for a year of underpaid work.

Despite the need for their labor, they were often looked on askance, suspected of being lazy, degenerate, and dirty, and of tending toward crimes of violence and passion. "Italians," complained a letter to the editor "render the neighborhood thoroughly undesirable for any other class of tenants." The New York police were particularly rough on them. Even Theodore Roosevelt, at about this time, declared publicly that Italians were less needed, less wanted, and less capable than the earlier immigrants, and definitely not assets to our country.

New arrivals from Italy were inured to life without plumbing, to being cold and hungry, and to sending their children out to work. What they were not used to were mechanical and other thunderous new noises, including torrents of loud abuse when they didn't understand English. Worst of all was life without relatives and loving neighbors, and without flowers and sunshine; and that was the life they were likely to find in the city. "Non c'è piacere nella vita" (there is no pleasure in life) was the opinion of many Italian immigrants, particularly the women. They were likely to find themselves living in tenements built according to the "dumbbell plan," which, strangely enough, had been chosen by the New York Health Department over two hundred other entries as the best arrangement for low-cost housing. The buildings' floor plan resembled a dumbbell, with four apartments on each floor—two at each end of the dumbbell. The narrowness in the middle accommodated a hallway, a watercloset, and a sink. Since families were apt to be large and also to take in boarders to help with the rent, there were frequently as many as forty persons using the facilities on each floor.

Fire laws were rudimentary as was insulation. By sheer luck, only one major fire occurred in New York during the blizzard, in a tenement on Mulberry Street. Fire engines were necessarily very slow in getting there; the fire chief came on a sled. Nearly a hundred people were left homeless, but there were no fatalities. How many slum residents died of disease, accident, or freezing during, or as a result of, the blizzard was not recorded.

People with little hope of a steady income might join a nebulous and ever shifting shantytown in uptown Manhattan. Wherever there were empty lots, squatters moved in and built hovels such as we see today in Manila or Rio de Janeiro. Downtown was for rent-payers, and it was unofficially but clearly divided into neighborhoods: Irish, German, Jewish, Italian, and black, as well as smaller enclaves for other groups who were less numerous. The neighborhoods changed gradually. For example, in 1888, blacks were living below Washington Square in decaying houses built about a century earlier by prosperous white merchants and businessmen. Over the next two or three decades, that neighborhood was to become Italian, and the blacks migrated uptown, eventually taking over Harlem. The section around the Manhattan entrance to the Great Bridge was, in 1888, an Irish preserve.

Alfred E. Smith grew up there and was fourteen years old at the time of the blizzard. (Forty years later, he would be running for president on the Democratic ticket.) He always looked back on his lower East Side childhood with affection.

What it lacked in luxury was made up for by the cheery mutual support of neighbors. In his memoir, he tells how people knew their alderman and counted on him in time of trouble. "Every funeral and every wake was attended by the whole neighborhood." In summer, the wagons that were always left overnight near the bridge and the ferry stations, while their owners and horses went home to Brooklyn, became a kind of general meeting place. Children played nearby or swam in the river (having learned to do so in the "fish cars"—holding tanks for fish and turtles at Fulton Market), while adults sat on the wagons and hashed over neighborhood news.

Al Smith's mother, a widow, supported her family by operating a small candy store in the basement of their house near the Great Bridge. Smith recalled that on Sunday evening "I put up the shutters [on the store] at ten o'clock. It was then misting rain. . . . When we awoke on the morning of March twelfth the candy store was buried under snow . . . we lost all track of it until midday on the following Tuesday."

Young Smith was a volunteer member of Engine Company Number 32. "In my after-school hours, for recreation, I practically lived in the engine house." When the blizzard set in, the company borrowed four sleighs from a leather company, but apparently did not need to use them.

On that frigid, lowering morning of Tuesday, March 13, young Smith, along with everyone else who lived within sight of the river, awoke to an amazing spectacle. From shore to shore, above and below the bridge, the river looked as if it were frozen. Since the East River is a saltwater tidal channel, it never freezes, but masses of ice, which gave it the look of a rough and uneven skating pond, had come down the Hudson during the night, entered the bay, and then, with the incoming tide, invaded the East River—a phenomenon that occurs maybe half a dozen times in a century. The last time had been only two years before, when the Reverend Henry Ward Beecher, with a flock of parishioners, had attempted to walk on the river from Brooklyn to New York and had had to be rescued as they were being carried off down the bay on a broken ice cake. On an earlier occasion, the ice had lasted several days, rising and falling as the tide beneath ran in and out. And in 1778, during the Revolution, when British troops were occupying New York, the entire upper bay became solidly iced over, and troops of Redcoats had marched across it from Staten Island, followed by wagon teams carrying supplies.

The ice this time was not a solid sheet, but a mosaic of broken floes jammed together, except for one huge chunk in the vicinity of the bridge, which stretched unbroken from Brooklyn to Manhattan. Watermen had a name for such a large piece of ice: "a harbor master."

When this huge floe was seen approaching, the ferries stayed in their slips. The floe was wider than the river. An edge of it scraped against the Mallory Steamship dock on the New York side and twisted several piles out of position. At the next pier, the Fulton Ferry Line, it boxed off the slips and jammed against a pier where an old-fashioned clipper ship was docked. At about the same moment, the floe jammed against docks on the Brooklyn side as well. One jagged edge pointed northward from the center, just under the bridge, and another point reached into the bay as far as Governor's Island. The whole floe covered many hundreds of acres.

Commuters to and from Brooklyn were now left waiting, in the bitter cold, for ferries that could not move from their slips. Many more were waiting to cross the Great Bridge, where traffic continued to be handled with great care and caution. On Monday no cable cars crossed it, partly because the bearing wheels of the cables were frozen stiff. By Tuesday morning this problem had been dealt with, but it was thought best to allow only one train to cross at a time. Each three-car train had two engines, one pushing, one pulling. The pedestrian walk had also been closed on Monday, because of the danger that the wind might blow people off. But now dense crowds were waiting to cross and were becoming very impatient. About eight o'clock the Brooklyn to Manhattan roadway was made available to pedestrians, and thousands immediately swarmed over it.

"Grown men frolicked like kittens and ran races," reported the *Sun*. "Eight young men procured a rope from somewhere and tied themselves to it and trotted across the bridge, pretending that they were enduring the perils of an ascent of the Alps." Later in the morning, seventy-five Italian workmen finished clearing a path on the pedestrian walk and it, too, was opened.

The following week, when storm damage to the city was being assessed, the Bridge Commission announced proudly that not the slightest vibration had been detected in the solid piers of the Great Bridge. Difficulties had all been due to snow, ice, and wind, not to any deficiency in the structure itself.

Bridge-crossers that morning could look down and see the river covered not only with ice but with pedestrians as well, running, sliding, hurrying, or cautiously picking their way along. Men and boys predominated, but there were women, too, and a number of dogs. Al Smith remembered seeing a harnessed horse swung onto the ice and ridden to Brooklyn by his owner. Not a few of those who saw all this happening forgot about getting to work and rushed out onto the river. Some of the dockworkers and the stormbound fishermen in the vicinity made the most of the situation by rigging ladders from the piers down to the ice and charging twenty-five cents or whatever the traffic would bear for the privilege of using them. And hordes of small boys, Smith among them, shinnied down the pilings and were among the first to slide and caper their way to Brooklyn across the awesome expanse. Even staid businessmen who had already reached their offices but found no business to transact could not resist dashing to the waterfront in order to make the historic trip.

One of them, a broker named Edward H. White, hustled down to the foot of Beekman Street and found himself in the midst of a great crowd of "gawkers," as he later said, all good-natured and having a fine time in spite of the intense cold. On the bridge, "immense crowds stood and gazed at the singular sight below." Mr. White, without even considering the danger, clambered down a ladder, and set forth for Brooklyn. "After about fifteen or twenty feet of rather hummocky ice, the rest was as even as a floor and it was an easy matter to walk. I went across almost to Martin's Stores in Brooklyn, and then for the first time in my excitement remembering my job, turned back and safely reached New York again."

Despite appearances, the crossing was certainly dangerous. In some places there was open water between the ice and the docks. Some crossers fell or were blown over by the wind, and had to be helped or carried to shore. Police on both sides of the river were trying to put a stop to it, but nevertheless, an estimated three thousand people made the trip. One observer noted that "the entrepreneurs with the ladders charged more to get people up from the ice than to let them go down."

While all this was going on, tugboats were arriving to try to break up the big floe. One of those hardworking *Sun* reporters was there, and wrote, "The powerful *Transfer No. 1* of the New Haven line went through the six-inch ice like cheese, to the second Fulton Ferry slip. This let the ferryboat *Fulton* start plying from Brooklyn." The owner of Martin's Stores, on the Brooklyn side, warned pedestrians away from his piers, saying the trip was "foolhardy." But they simply moved on to the next pier. Charles Peck, of Brooklyn, crossed twice; his wife had been the first woman to cross the Brooklyn Bridge, and he was eager to outdo her. Another man said that the wind blew him clear across without effort on his part and he wished the ice were permanent. And an energetic dog belonging to a Brooklyn junk dealer was observed to scamper shore to shore four times.

The tugboats made little progress until the tide turned at 9:46 A.M., and the effect became noticeable about fifteen minutes later. The average citizen did not know what was going to happen, but seamen did, and they warned people away from the ladders.

"Very many refused to obey," said the *Sun*. "When the ladders were taken away, they let themselves down from the piers. . . . They thirsted for glory." Some had to be physically restrained by longshoremen.

"At the turn of the tide the great icefield moved. Not a crack on the surface showed the change, but a grating upon the ends of the piers against which it was pinned told the story to the self-appointed watchers. There were over a hundred persons on the ice at this moment. Most of them broke into a run. Others plodded along at their own time, the surface seeming firm. . . . Loud were the cries [from those watching] to get to the shore. . . . After several minutes, with some quick creaking and cracking from end to end, the floe began to shift seaward. The most imperturbable then took fright."

Some forty people were still on the big ice floe as it floated toward Black Ball dock, on the Manhattan side, where most of them had begun their adventure. But the floe did not stop moving. Instead, it shifted seaward. Some of the stranded made a grab at the end of the Fulton Ferry pier, but the edges of the ice no longer seemed solid and the pilings were slippery. All forty crowded to the side of the floe nearest land. "Some laughed. . . . Some exchanged cool jokes with those on the docks. One quietly asked to have a tug sent down for him; another requested a stove; still another shouted that he'd cable from Europe. . . . One man sank down on his knees and prayed.

"Several tugs began to get up steam for the rescue, but the floe grated against the Mallory piers—crumbled and shivered and almost stopped. The pause was only for five minutes, but in that time a score of dock employees lowered ladders and helped everyone ashore. One man in his nervousness reeled to one side and slid off into the icy water. The longshoremen were nearby, and quickly seized him and pulled him out. Another man was found covered with ice from head to foot. His teeth chattered, his eyes were dull, his face was white. He said he'd broken through some rotten ice on the Brooklyn edge of the floe and been hauled up on the form ice. People had told him to go ashore, but he said he'd cross that river if he died for it." He almost did.

After that, the floe, without passengers, moved on rapidly, but on the Brooklyn side a new drama had developed. Three men had been just starting across when the turning tide caused a tug suddenly to plunge forward through the ice, cutting it "like piecrust," and to bear down upon the three young men.

"The men stopped in terror," continued the *Sun*. "The ice bulged underneath them with the pressure and the waves. Had they rushed on they would at least have stood upon the main sheet. As it was they hesitated, moved back, forward, back, and stood still. The ice cracked merrily. Then it bulged up, separated and each young man was launched upon a separate cake of ice. The tug had gone through like an arrow and was far upstream. The men shouted frantically and waved their arms. So did the crowds. Several tugs saw and started to the rescue, but the ice intervened. Two of the men were on neighboring ice cakes. One finally made a dangerous jump to the cake nearer the shore on which the other stood. The crowd shouted approval, told them to keep their hearts.

"The other young man, who was irreproachably dressed and carried a satchel, was on a cake scarcely twenty-five feet in diameter. He ran from edge to edge, till each time he nearly dipped in the water, and showed such terror that terror was communicated to those on shore."

As the cakes drifted near Roberts' Stores, in Brooklyn, men on the piers tried to throw lines to the men. It was only fifty feet, but the wind spoiled their aim. The men drifted farther away and their cries redoubled. The tug *James Watt* approached and threw them lines, but failed to connect. Finally the tug *S. E. Babcock* got near enough for Captain Elisha Morris to haul them over the rail. Shouts went up from the shore and the tug steamed toward the Battery.

"A fourth man was caught at the same time, but being near the shore, he threw himself in the water and was pulled up on the docks."

Near the Manhattan side, there were three castaways on a cake "as big as Washington Square" and two each on cakes "the size of door mats." A tug pushed the big cake slowly to the wharf and the men leaped off. Then the tug went after the door mats, which were now floating rapidly into the bay, came around to intercept them, and plucked the men off. "The thousands of men on the riverside and the Bridge yelled their applause in rounds of cheers and screams."

———

In the crowds that hovered around the bridge that day, watching the excitement, ragged newsboys hawked their papers. A kind woman who kept a shop nearby had wrapped the heads of several of them in cotton batting, for warmth, which gave the boys the look of battle-wounded. The newspapers sold fast, as they contained the first news of the blizzard. The Monday papers had been a disappointment, not even mentioning the weather but going on at great length about the death of Kaiser Wilhelm I in Berlin, and the elaborate funeral he was to have. In France, the Panama Canal Company had failed, to the distress of 800,000 stockholders; in Rome, Pope Leo XIII was making plans for a jubilee year. There was a strike on the Chicago, Burlington and Quincy Railroad; and in Richmond, Virginia, they were tearing down the old slave pen. Such news was written for people sitting comfortably at breakfast tables or speeding toward their offices on trains, els, and ferries. For blizzard sufferers, it had minimal interest, as did the little poem that had appeared in the Monday morning *Herald*:

The First Dandelion

Simple and fresh and fair from winter's close emerging,
As if no artifice of fashion, business, politics, had ever been.
Forth from its sunny nook of shelter'd grace—innocent, golden, calm
    as the dawn,
The spring's first dandelion shows its trustful face.
                    WALT WHITMAN

On Wednesday morning, *Herald* readers found the following riposte:

The First Blizzard

Simple and fresh and fierce, from Winter's clothes emerging
As if no artifice of summer, business, politics, had ever been,

Forth from its snowy nook of shivering glaciers—innocent, silver, pale
  as the dawn,
The Spring's first blizzard shows its wryful face.

AFTER WALT WHITMAN

The Tuesday *Times*, first on the streets, had sensibly moved
the kaiser's funeral to an inside page. Its headline read

IN A BLIZZARD'S GRASP
THE WORST STORM THE CITY
HAS EVER KNOWN

The snow that fell all Tuesday afternoon seemed heavier
than it was, because the wind seized it and whirled it about
with dust. Most people who had struggled to and from work
the day before stayed home, many of them sick in bed. Those
who had not ventured out on Monday mistook a brief morning
appearance of the sun for the end of the storm and went to
work, only to find doors locked and telegraph wires silent. Els
were moving on a curtailed schedule and with short trains, and
the stations were an even colder ordeal than they had been on
Monday. Car windows were heavily frosted, and the passengers
might as well have been traveling through an Arctic whiteout.

Shops and school buildings were hemmed in by drifts that
towered twenty to thirty feet high, with similar ranges piled
between barely shoveled sidewalks and the streets. A shoveling
detail, cleaning an el platform, was arrested for dumping snow
into the street. They were taken before a judge, who scolded
them severely, but had no answer to the question of where else
they could have put it. The police ordered all building occu-
pants and owners to clean their sidewalks, a disagreeable prospect in view of the cold and the still-falling snow. Those who
could afford it hired some of the Italians away from el and
horsecar lines, paying them double or triple.

148

"Women are rather more plenty in the streets than on Monday," the *Sun* said, "and they get along a great deal better. They attracted a great deal of attention and deserve it, for rosy is but a poor term to describe their complexions, and sparkling is only a weak word to indicate the brightness of their eyes."

Cabs had become somewhat easier to find, and some drivers had substituted sleighs; but the wind and temperature were too cold for sleighing as a sport. The parks lay with unbroken white expanses, and thousands of side streets, especially in outlying sections, were almost as pristine. Postmen, who had had a frightful time on Monday, now had very little mail to deliver, and none from out of town. They stopped in front of each house and bawled for people to come out and get their letters if they wanted them, or to let down a basket on a rope. Brownstone stoops were drifted to the tops of doors and parlor windows, and householders kept gaslights burning all day long. Insulation in older houses was very often deficient, and the back window of one frail wooden house at Madison Avenue and 130th Street actually blew in, allowing ice and frozen snow to invade both back and front parlors. The children put on their skates and frolicked around the furniture, while solid sheets of ice formed over the broken window.

At the Stock Exchange, fifty brokers turned up and eighteen hundred shares were traded, but the telegraph was still out. According to the *Sun*, "they wandered over the echoing floor of the great Board room. Most of those on hand hadn't been home over night. . . . There was a dreary effort by some of the alleged wits to make things pleasant." Using the floor of the exchange as a ball park, "Half a dozen played 'one-old cat,' the baseball game of their boyhood." Deliveries of stocks and loan accommodations were again extended twenty-four hours. And, as on Monday, the exchange closed early.

East River ferries were crippled by the ice jam, but on the

Hudson most ferries were in business, even though the river was as choppy as a sea and made dangerous by great chunks of wave-tossed ice.

The horsecar lines were still shut down. Although the companies were losing daily receipts of thirty thousand dollars, shoveling out would have cost more than that. "Cheaper to wait for a thaw," a stockholder told the *World*, or wait for city street-cleaners, whichever came first. The superintendent of horsecars said, "We're coming to life as soon as any of 'em, but no one can tell when that's going to be." He added that they had 250 men out shoveling, some of them horsecar conductors and drivers, and the rest Italians. The frozen slush on the tracks had to be chopped away with pickaxes, and the whole effort was very slowgoing.

"I have been in this business since there was first a horsecar," one elderly conductor was quoted as saying, "and I never before knew it to be necessary to use picks on the road." Much of the trouble was caused by the ice formed early on Monday morning, when the rain had turned to snow. It was still there, underneath everything else. When, on Tuesday evening, the tracks were cleared from Grand Central down to 23rd Street and the cars began to operate, "people cheered them as they went."

Here and there all over town the horsecars abandoned on Monday were still encumbering the streets. But many were no longer abandoned. The homeless and the stranded had moved into them, keeping up fires in the little car stoves and even doing a bit of cooking. One group enlivened their sojourn with a considerable amount of beer, borrowed from a beer truck abandoned nearby.

A driver named Walter Hall told a *Sun* reporter that his boss had said to him on Monday morning, "Take the horses and go down as far as you can." He had started out on his regular route, from 99th Street to the Battery, and "half the time I was on the tracks and half the time I was over on the curb. But I stuck it out as far as the Bowery. There I stopped my poor horses and I opened the door and I said to the passengers, 'this is as far as this car goes!' I sent the horses back to the 14th Street barn by a boy."

All Mr. Hall's "fares" meekly got out—"all except one woman who sat at the far end of the car with a big bundle in her lap. There she sat crying. I stepped up to her and said, 'What's the matter? Bad news from home?' She said, 'No, I hain't, but I gave you the last nickel I had and I've got to take this washing down to the Battery.' So I grabbed up the washing . . . I cut the bell strap (I wasn't going to have anyone ringing up fares on me). I gave her a quarter and turned her over to a cop who took her to the el on the Bowery and helped her up the stairs.

"Then I got some coal in the neighborhood and filled up the boxes underneath the seats so I'd have plenty. Stayed there Tuesday to Friday. On the first night, after I'd stretched out on the seat, two fellers banged on the door, wanted to come in. They had a keg of beer with them. I said, 'You can come in if you behave yourselves.' They said they had a load of beer out there they had to guard, so they'd behave. So there we three stayed from Tuesday to Friday, living on beer and pretzels."

Friends and admirers of the late Henry Bergh, founder of the ASPCA, were eager to give him a fine funeral, but there was no way of knowing when it might take place. His body lay at home, cooled by tubs of ice, until an undertaker could take it away. And this was the case with hundreds of people who had died at home since Saturday. Bereaved families who had managed to hold a funeral on Monday morning and had then attempted to go to the cemetery were in an even worse plight.

Some had to abandon the hearse in the middle of a road. Others got part way to a cemetery—most cemeteries were in semirural areas—and then were able to persuade a farmer to keep the hearse and coffin in his barn until they could come back for them; or perhaps they found a kind householder willing to accommodate a dead body for a night or two. One woman was traumatized for years by seeing a hearse overturn, the coffin spill out of the hearse, and the body fall out of the coffin.

If it was a bad week for dying, it was not very good for passing other important milestones of life. L. B. Aspen, fourteen, was reporting for his first job on Monday. "I did not want to take a chance of losing it," he said later. So he walked from his home on East 43rd Street to the lower tip of Manhattan. "Jobs those days were hard to get—even office boy jobs. I worked in that office for thirty-two years and became the company's secretary."

A baby whose name and fate we don't know was born on one of the el trains, stalled at the height of the storm. The few women on board made a circle around the mother as she gave birth on the frigid and filthy floor.

The Thurman family of Brooklyn was scheduled to move on March 12 to a new house. "All movable articles already boxed or barreled, the stove and pipes taken down ... No moving that day!" as one of the Thurmans remembered many years later. "Put up the stove again, broke up some boxes for firewood and melted snow for water.... There were four smaller children in the house than I. The following day, Dad and I fought our way to Newton Creek coal yards with my small sled and secured a bag of coal."

Mr. and Mrs. Joseph McIntyre had been married the week before. McIntyre stayed home from work all week, and said he "enjoyed every minute of it." Other newlyweds who thought well of the blizzard were Mr. and Mrs. William Sittenham.

They were spending their honeymoon at a small boardinghouse in Dutchess County, New York, from which there was no possibility of departure for more than a week. Venturing out on Wednesday, they discovered that the village store was unusually well supplied with fireworks, especially rockets.

"I'd like some fireworks," Mr. Sittenham said.

"What kind?"

"Every kind."

"How many?"

"All of them."

With deep snow in every direction and little danger of fire, the Sittenhams set off box after box of fireworks, lighting up the cold night landscape with high-soaring symbols of their feelings.

By nightfall of Tuesday, March 13, the situation on the railroads had hardly changed since the day before. Trains that got stuck on Monday were still stuck, and the only change was that the passengers had become more miserable. In most cases, some sort of food had reached them, so they were not starving, but they were certainly cold and had burned up anything that would burn in the car stoves, including the furniture. "Sanitation is worsening," the newspapers reported, leaving details to the reader's imagination. It was a lift to the spirits to have singers and musicians aboard; although on a train stalled near Jersey City a troupe called the Lilly Clay Blondes locked themselves into a Pullman and refused to come out until rescued. In contrast, on a train four miles out of Schenectady a Pullman porter played the harmonica, banjo, and triangle—a one-man band.

On Monday, the passengers on another upstate train had consumed all the caramels and dried figs in the trainboy's basket, and on Tuesday morning had nothing to eat. "Some of the more athletic passengers" walked half a mile to a house and persuaded an elderly couple to sell them what food they could spare: half a mince pie, a pound of cheese, four hard sandwiches, and six cookies "made almost entirely of lard and flour." They also reached an isolated farmhouse inhabited by a family of German immigrants, who turned out to be more in need of help than the passengers. The whole family was sleeping in one bed; there was no heat, and nothing to eat except hardtack and a few potatoes. The train was rescued late Wednesday; the German family, probably never.

As snowplows and work trains loaded with shovelers began to move out, there were accidents. In New Jersey, a trackman's train ran into a snowbank with such force that the collision shattered the glass in the headlights and cab windows, injuring the engineer. Chopping the frozen drifts with axes was backbreaking work. Sledgehammers had to be used to move switches. And at Trenton, a relief train ran into a stalled commuter train that had fortunately just been emptied of passengers. The cars telescoped, derailed, and caught fire from a stove.

Hundreds of commuters spent three days in the Long Island Railroad terminal. "The lingering hope that perhaps a train would move out kept the crowd in the station," said the *Times*. None moved out, but a rescue train came in, bearing the president of the railroad, who had been plucked from a stalled train near Babylon. The sight of him seemed to hearten the crowd, and they cheered.

Scores of stockcars were marooned in the New York Central yards at Albany. All day Monday and Tuesday, the city heard the cries of suffering animals—especially the hogs. Many died of thirst and hunger, if not of freezing. Unofficial estimates of perishable-food losses on the New York Central alone came to ten million dollars.

———

Back at the New York City Weather Service, late Tuesday, the roof began to leak. The ever-resourceful staff—Sergeant Long included, no doubt—sopped up the puddles with large sponges.

WEDNESDAY, MARCH 14

Wednesday,
March 14

COULD the great storm really be ending? Higher temperatures (rising to 39° in mid-afternoon) and some wan sunshine seemed to suggest it. GOODBYE BLIZZARD was one cheery headline. THE STORM PASSING AND THE ELEVATED ROAD STRUGGLING INTO MOTION.

A kind of zany humor—nineteenth-century style—arose among the blizzard-struck population. Perhaps it began with just one jokester being inspired to put a comical sign on top of the snowdrift that barricaded his house or shop, and the idea spread. Or perhaps to place a funny sign on a snowdrift just seemed the logical thing to do in such crazy times. A florist stuck his snowdrift full of unsold flowers, with a sign that said, Don't Pick the Flowers. On a roof-high drift, a purveyor of house paint wrote, Now Is the Time to Paint Your Roof. A restaurant, closed because no one could get through the drift that blocked its front door, posted a gloomy message: No Heat, No Food, No Nothin'. And a bank topped off its mammoth snowbank with, This Bank Is Closed Indefinitely.

Other wits wrote, Perishable Property ... It Is Better to See the Rain Rain Than the Snow Reign ... Do You Get My Drift? ... This Way to the Klondike ... Nobody's Claim ... Don't Touch This Snow, It's All We've Got ... It's Snow Joke ... Make Us an Offer ... Wanted—a Cashier for This Bank ... This Lot to Be Raffled July 4. Chances $10 ... Snow for Sale! Come Early and Avoid the Rush! ... Take Some!

A clergyman on a train stalled in a cut was inspired to tell his fellow passengers, "This is the most unkindest cut."

Practical jokes must have been hard to bear at such a time, but on Eighth Avenue, in New York, two boys full of excess energy dug a seventy-five-foot path that led pedestrians around a corner into a dead end.

All this may have helped take people's minds off very serious matters, such as injuries, loss of revenue, destruction of property, and—most critical of all—shortages of food and fuel. With shops unable to open and supply trains failing to reach the city, shortages worsened hourly. The poor had no emergency supplies laid by, having only enough money to buy food and fuel every day.

In the tenements, milk was customarily delivered door to door well before dawn. A milkman with a large can in one hand and a lantern in the other (tenements usually were lit by only one gas jet on every other floor), groped through the dreary hallways in the hours before dawn, pouring milk into pails left hanging on doorknobs. The milk was thin and blue, and often adulterated with chalk and with minute evil objects, such as insects, mouse hair, and all manner of bacteria. But, when boiled, it was better than no milk at all, and for countless city babies it meant survival. Most cheap milk came from cows that spent their lives in dirty, sunless barns within the city limits, but even this had not been distributed since Monday. Meat was scarce as well, and so was seafood and the ingredients needed for making bread.

People can go hungry for weeks without dying, but they cannot remain chilled for long. The coal shortage was the most dangerous. A few public-spirited dealers who were well supplied, sold coal at the usual price and even gave it away to those who couldn't pay. On the lower East Side, the proprietor of a Russian-Turkish bath decided to close the establishment and give his coal to anyone who needed it. Others charged outrageous prices. A man who worked for a West 8th Street grocer never forgot that his boss had ordered him to charge a dollar for a pail of coal, which usually cost ten cents. He rejoiced when someone stole the wheels off the grocer's wagon, which was stuck in the street, and replaced them with old ones, leaving a chalked message, Fair Exchange Is No Robbery.

On 10th Street at the corner of Broadway, Louis Fleischmann's Vienna Model Bakery was in the habit of giving away leftover bread and rolls every evening. During the blizzard days, the bakery stayed open through the night, dispensing baked goods to people who otherwise might have gone hungry. All through Tuesday night, beside the elegant Gothic spires of Grace Church, and across the street from the most elaborate department store in town, originally A. T. Stewart's, long lines of men, women, and children wound around the block and back again.

Early on Wednesday morning, crowds of housewives converged upon the coal bins in front of grocery stores—so many that policemen hovered nearby in case things got out of hand. Even at exorbitant prices signs soon appeared in grocery windows: Coal All Out.

The *World* wrote, "Women, bareheaded and scantily clothed, dragging shivering children at their heels and carrying little tin pails burst into tears on reading the placards and turned away to pursue an all too often equally fruitless search at other stores."

And yet there was no looting. Arrests for stealing from groceries or other stores were fewer than usual. Even when a coal cart broke down in full view of tenement windows, and its driver, in despair, was about to leave it unguarded and take his horses to the stable, there was no stealing. Instead, "fully a hundred women and girls with pails and baskets and tin cans swarmed around the coal cart clamoring for the coal. In less than five minutes it was all sold. The load brought over $7."

Dealers lucky enough to have coal on hand found it next to impossible to transport. Some of them hired men to deliver bags of coal on their backs. One resourceful dealer hammered packing boxes together and put them on runners.

In normal times, a great deal of food, varying in quality from very good to terrible, was available in the cities. The prosperous could count on fresh vegetables from the South during most of the year. Dressed meat came from Chicago in refrigerator cars, and New Yorkers were said to consume an average of a pound of meat per capita daily (compared to half a pound daily in London, and three-quarters of a pound in Paris). The reported East Coast consumption of oysters seems incredibly high: New York City alone daily accounted for seventy-five thousand baskets of oysters, with two hundred in each basket: fifteen million oysters.

Although refrigerator cars were in common use by 1888, most of New York's meat still arrived on the hoof and was either slaughtered and processed in abattoirs or sold live at open markets. Butchers and private individuals were allowed to slaughter animals themselves and throw the offal into the gutters. Meat carcasses hung outside butcher shops, where, in warm weather, swarms of flies, breeding in the abundant horse manure in the streets, had a feast. Food consumed by the poor was nearly always of dubious quality, anyway. Even when it was not exposed to flies, or to mice, rats, and cockroaches, it was full of impurities and adulterated. There was no Food and Drug Administration, and recommendations of the city's Health Department did not carry much weight, as some of its members were believed to be open to bribes from business interests. In response to citizens' complaints about the vile smells in the streets—sewer gas, illuminating gas, dead animals, and other things that made New Yorkers welcome a brisk sea breeze—the Health Department replied that smells were "not detrimental to health, but only destructive of comfort," and that to forbid them would be to cause commercial distress. And when a group of doctors pointed out that children of the poor contracted fatal illnesses from playing in the streets and gutters, the answer was that the children had better play elsewhere.

Mayor Hewitt, who had been able to get to City Hall on Monday and Tuesday via the Third Avenue el ("pretty well squeezed on the way," the *World* said), got there the same way on Wednesday, and conferred with the Superintendent of Streets and Roads about snow removal. For the duration of the emergency, snow was to be dumped from any pier instead of the usual few. A committee of merchants called upon the mayor and offered to clean certain downtown streets, well aware, no doubt, that if they didn't do it themselves the city might not do it for weeks. The job was certainly daunting. Priority was given to Broadway and other main thoroughfares that were not only heavily drifted but clogged with fallen utility poles and wires.

Garbage collection would have to wait, but that was nothing new. Many a householder, impatient with the city's desultory service, was in the habit of paying a man with a dogcart to take garbage away. But this week the rickety two-wheeled carts, each drawn by one melancholy mongrel, could not get through the drifts, and the only way to dispose of garbage was to burn it in the kitchen stove.

The Blizzard of '88 made New Yorkers painfully aware of the inadequacy of their sanitation facilities, and within a few years the entire system was overhauled. Instead of hiring itiner-

163

ant laborers by the hour, the city established a permanent force that swept and cleaned the streets daily. New ordinances forbade coal bins, sheds, and other impedimenta on the sidewalks. The street cleaners wore white uniforms and once a year put on a parade down Fifth Avenue, marching with their brooms proudly held like muskets.

"The Army of the Shovel" now organized by the Superintendent of Streets and Roads could not get around as fast as everyone had hoped. Wagons began to move, but many were soon stuck again, creating terrible traffic jams. Pedestrians could use the south side of cross streets without much trouble, but the north sides were still overwhelmed with giant drifts. Householders on the north paid shovelers five dollars to clear their walks and steps; while on the south, the going rate was no more than seventy-five cents.

"Those who started gaily out with fresh horses," observed one newspaper, "and the comfortable consciousness that the storm was over were speedily undeceived as to their expectations of getting anywhere. A block or two of travelling would use up the horse or horses, and one or two experiences of digging a way through drifts would use up the driver. Few truckmen attempted to get out their teams and those who did were soon obliged to relinquish them."

On Wednesday afternoon, sleighs began to come out. In the old days, before the advent of horsecar tracks, Broadway had always been gay with sleigh-riders after a snowstorm. Now the snow was deep and hard-packed enough to cover the tracks, and the street was soon thronged with cutters and sledges and elaborate private sleighs. Plumes adorned the horses' heads and the hats of the riders. In Central Park, a lady in sables drove a handsome Russian sleigh along an unbroken roadway—"bravado and a desire for sensation," commented the *World*. Women, it went on, should not go out at all in this weather unless absolutely necessary.

"Pedestrians were plenty," noted the Wednesday *Sun*. "The air was more bracing, and the absence of flying clouds of snowy particles fine as fog" was a great improvement over Tuesday. Improvised blizzard clothing was still being worn. "A soft hat tied down over the ears with a handkerchief was a prevailing mode, and coarse packing cord tied tightly about the trousers at the ankle was the correct caper in west side high life. A few extremists, who sported rubber boots to their knees, were scorned as dudes. Coarse bagging or brown packing paper tied about the feet and legs was good enough for ordinary folks like grocers' boys and butchers' assistants." As for the ladies, "a hood drawn close, and a peaked expression of countenance, were the observable features of most female costumes."

Getting rid of the snow so that normal life might resume was a problem that beset every town and city in the Northeast. Property owners lit fires inside huge drifts, which did the trick but caused serious flooding of gutters and basements. And they excavated tunnels through drifts, Arctic passageways with gray daylight filtering into them, eerie and not very safe. A unique solution to road-clearing was contributed in New Jersey by a breeder of Saint Bernards who put ten of his dogs to work running back and forth to break a road to the railroad station.

In Liberty, New York, a farmer who finally reached his barn found six head of young cattle standing on their feet but drifted entirely with snow, so that only their heads were visible. Yet they had survived. Their owner photographed them and then plunged off in snow up to his armpits to record other strange things, such as the railroad station with its roof off. Standing on the top of a snowdrift, he and his camera were level with the chimney top of a two-and-a-half story house. He photographed a twenty-foot drift and then, in June, recorded the last remnants of it, by that time a meager lump of white among the grass and apple blossoms.

Chauncey Depew was no longer smiling, but he had been at his desk at Grand Central every day of the blizzard. Late on Wednesday, a wan smile was in order. A train that had left Albany that morning actually pulled into the terminal, five hours late, bringing 150 passengers. A train from New York to Albany also arrived five hours late—on the southbound track. A dozen or more of the missing state legislators were aboard. These successful trips showed that the shovel gangs had cleared one track through the Fourth Avenue tunnel and on the main line. But to clear the entire tunnel would take another forty-eight hours, and the Connecticut line would not move for another three days. Nearly all of the passengers stranded on that line had by now been taken off the cars by sleigh. At South Norwalk, Connecticut, an eighteen-year-old passenger on one of those stalled trains volunteered to help the crew by shoveling. Later he got a check from the railroad company for sixty cents—his wage for several hours' labor.

A gang of two hundred shovelers at Meriden, Connecticut, had the temerity to demand a raise, from 27½ cents to 50 cents an hour. They got it, because of the absolute need for their services; however, when the news reached headquarters in New York, it caused considerable headshaking.

Farther south, three trains arrived in Washington from Philadelphia, reporting that the track was still badly obstructed by drifts and fallen telegraph poles. The nation's capital had only five wires open, two to the south and three to the west.

Richard Spamer, a passenger from St. Louis, had a tale to tell about his trip to New York on a Baltimore and Ohio train that had been due into the New Jersey terminal on Monday evening. He left St. Louis on Saturday. East of Pittsburgh, the train encountered a snowstorm, and finally stalled somewhere in the Alleghenies. All day Spamer and six other passengers in a Pullman car sat in reasonable comfort, with coffee and sandwiches served by dining-car stewards, watching the snow "not falling directly but all day blown horizontally past the windows." Food ran out by evening, and there was no steam. The driving gear of the locomotive was a solid mass of ice. The crew—engineer, conductor, fireman, and porters—all joined the passengers in the stove-heated Pullman to spend the night. Next morning a relief party arrived with hampers of sandwiches and pots of coffee, but as there was no hope of moving the train the passengers left it and found their way up the track to a small hotel. On Saturday the train got underway, passengers and crew reembarked, and completed their journey on Sunday. Spamer's account of the trip, as told to the New York *World*, was the first post-blizzard news telegraphed to St. Louis directly from New York.

Newspaper reporters were out in droves, looking for exciting stories. The *World* published a special blizzard edition on Wednesday afternoon. The price was twenty-five cents instead of the usual two, but the whole edition sold out quickly. Kaiser Wilhelm's funeral was not even mentioned.

Because of the slow repair of telegraph lines, every city had to make the most of local news, since little was known about other places. In New Haven, the *Register* catalogued all sorts of events, some not very exciting: "Many ladies took a ride on the cars to see the big snow banks along the route . . . A man drove through the center of New Haven in a flat-bottomed rowboat drawn by a single horse. He sat calmly in the stern and glided smoothly over drift and shallow . . . J. S. Alley and about a hundred of his neighbors broke a road from Orange Center and brought about one thousand quarts of milk."

From Washington via Chicago came the news that "the proceedings of Congress have been quite as dull as for any preceding week of the session," and that bluebirds had arrived, along with hundreds of robins on the Capitol grounds. In eastern Virginia, there were floods, and an entire island was submerged, taking with it a large herd of cattle that had been wintering there.

In Philadelphia, a snowplow drawn by twenty-eight horses still could not break through the drifts without a gang shoveling in front of it.

Three reporters from the Providence *Journal* set out to reach the train stranded at Saybrook. They got as far as Niantic, and there, against all advice, set forth in a sleigh. They soon found no railroad tracks at all to follow, nothing but "one great sheet of snow covering everything from sight, save the tops of the walls and fences, the brush and trees and scattered farmhouse." They saw no one, even peeking out of windows.

After a conference, they decided to send the sleigh and horses back to New London. Then they walked cross-country until they found some railroad tracks, which they followed to the village of Lyme. Shovel brigades had been through the cuts, but the heaped-up snow they left behind had caved in and the going was hard. The reporters walked on the tracks, using fence rails to balance themselves like tightrope walkers. At the village of Blackhall they tried to hire a horse and sleigh, but with no success. "The people knew nothing of what had been going on outside their little hamlet and had settled down for the rain or some enterprising person to come along and dig them out. Nothing would tempt them to hitch up a horse and sleigh. . . . They looked out and saw an ocean of snow, and that settled it."

The only food the reporters could buy was, curiously enough, oranges; a surprising treat here in the middle of this trans-planted Arctic. Then they returned to the tracks and kept walking, sometimes having to pull each other through drifts. They hoped to hitch a ride on a work train, but they arrived in Lyme before they saw any train, and were too exhausted to go farther.

At Lyme, they found the W. C. Turner Comedy Company, a vaudeville troupe. To while away the time, one of the comedi-ans had brought a rifle and was "blazing away at gulls." Most readers of the Providence *Journal* may have found the reporters' story lacking in drama, but perhaps a few of them relished the fantastic, surreal charm of the vast white setting, the oranges, the indifferent country folk, and the comedian firing at the sea gulls.

In Brooklyn, the city editor of the *Eagle* sent Richard C. Reilly, a twenty-one-year-old cub reporter, to find out whether the Brighton Beach Hotel at Coney Island really had blown away, as rumored. By alternately walking and hitching rides, Reilly reached Coney Island on Wednesday afternoon, and found the hotel firmly anchored where it had always been (later that year it was moved back because of the erosion of the beach). Reilly then rented a one-horse sleigh and started home. Al-though he was wearing two sets of clothing, he was cold, and he stopped at several saloons along the way to take a warming glass. That may have been his undoing. He was found next morning at six by a passing farmer—upright in the driver's seat, still holding the reins of the frozen horse, but uncon-scious. The farmer took him to the nearest hospital, where all his extremities were found to be frozen. He was still alive, but the treatment—hot bricks applied directly to his body—may have killed him. He died on Friday.

The pilot schooner *Caldwell F. Colt,* on which the *World* reporter William O. Inglis had so lightheartedly embarked on Saturday, had been lying hove to on Tuesday night, and at daybreak on Wednesday made sail "as well as the ice would allow," and headed for port. "We all thanked God that we were alive," Inglis wrote. "Mr. Fairgreaves [the acting captain] said he had been to sea and sailed all over the world for the past 34 years and had never seen such a hurricane."

The bay was scattered with wrecked schooners and with tugs bringing in heavily damaged vessels. Other schooners were caught in the ice along the shore, and tugs hovered near them, hoping for jobs. "We saw three wrecked pilot-boats ashore in the Horseshoe back of Sandy Hook, another in Gravesend, and poor No. 2, with nothing but her masts showing as she sank below the Bay Ridge pier. The American ensign, union down, still fluttered apeak of her mainmast. Everybody saw these things, but no one felt like saying anything about them."

The hungry crew went below for dinner, having been unable to sit down to a hot meal since Sunday. "As we fell to sharply, a tug passed by one quarter to windward. The man at the wheel hailed her for news.

" 'Nine pilot boats wrecked,' was the answer and we could all hear it. Big Fairgreaves pushed his plate away and went on deck. There were tears coming out of the corners of his eyes. None of the rest of us ate any more."*

Later, when the true damages were assessed, it was found that the news was not so bad. The *Phantom* and the *Enchantress*

*William O. Inglis went on to a fine career in journalism. After fifteen years on the *World*, he went to *Harper's Weekly*, wrote on foreign relations, and published two books. During the 1920s, he worked with John D. Rockefeller on papers for the Rockefeller archives. He was also a founder of the Silurians (a society of veteran newspapermen). He died in 1949 at the age of eighty-seven.

had indeed vanished for good. The *W. H. Starbuck* had been in collision with a fruit steamer from the Mediterranean at the height of the storm and then, with her bowsprit and mainsail carried away and her bulwarks in splinters, she had been swept helplessly a hundred miles out to sea. On the following Saturday, she was sighted off Barnegat Bay, on the south New Jersey coast, by a revenue cutter, the *U. S. Grant*. The captain declined the *Grant*'s help, saying that his schooner was not taking on water and there were others in greater need of help.

The *Grant* then hailed the pilot boat *James G. Bennett*, which had been at the Delaware breakwater. She was in tow and taking water, but her captain also declined assistance. One of her pilots had nearly lost his life when a British bark foundered after he had boarded her. But the wrecked bark was hauled in by tugs and all aboard survived.

Next, the *Grant* cruised down the Jersey coast to check on the Cape May lightship. She was still there. The *Grant*'s captain wrapped newspapers concerning the blizzard around a stick and threw them to the lightship keeper. They fell into the sea, but the keeper immediately lowered a boat to pick them up.

On Sunday evening five New York pilot boats had taken refuge inside the horseshoe at Sandy Hook. One of their captains said later, "A few coasting schooners, bound east, were at anchor in the bend, and others were coming in for a harbor. Most of them anchored pretty close to the west shore of Sandy Hook so as to ride in smooth water. None of them expected the wind to jump round to the westward and blow great guns like it did before midnight, putting them all too close to a lee shore." The vessels were soon driven into the breakers. "The spray froze on their rigging and each sea swept their decks and poured below. Knocked down repeatedly by the wind and sea, the men yet managed to fire guns of distress, which were heard by the life-saving crew on shore. . . . During three hours of fearful suspense the half-frozen crews heard the surf getting closer astern every moment. They knew that with every inch of cable out their splendid craft were dragging their anchors and must soon strike the beach. Oil bags were hung over the bows and they smoothed the great ground swell combers a little but not enough to save them.

"The stern of the *Williams* struck the beach first. The first sea turned her broadside on to the beach and broke high over her port side. Pilots and crew jumped overboard when she struck. The yawls were useless and it was a swim for life. Encumbered by heavy clothes, oilers, and rubber boots, it was a wonder they reached the shore, but they did, swimming, wading, and then crawling half drowned up the icy beach. These men again faced almost certain death in a half-mile tramp to the boarding house across the peninsula kept by Mrs. Stuart. Supporting Pilot Marshall White, who otherwise would have fallen by the wayside, they reached the house by sheer luck two hours later.

"The crew of the *Blunt* managed to beach the ship and were able to jump to the sand without having to swim. The *Story* was thrown ashore broadside. Some of the crew reached safety in the yawl and others had to swim." They, too, reached Mrs. Stuart's boardinghouse, and so did other castaways. One was a captain's wife from a fishing sloop, with her feet and legs so frozen that they would have to be amputated. Other crews were rescued by the lifesavers on shore who put planks out over the ice. (It was ice that had come from the Hudson, and the shallow water was littered with it.) In all, that day, fifty seamen were saved from death at Sandy Hook.

Down at Lewes, Delaware, the Bay was also a mass of ice and the shore was strewn with vessels. Crowds of bystanders lounged about, fascinated, staring at the two-hundred-foot-wide gaps in the pier, which had been made by the colliding *Crawford* and *Tamesei*. Stranded sailors haunted the waterfront, boarding their ships if they could. According to the laws concerning shipwrecks, the consignees got any salvaged cargo and the owners the vessels, while the crews depended on the sale value of rigging, anchors, sails, and other parts of the ships in order to reclaim their wages.

Immigrants arriving at the portals of that golden land where everything always went right, suddenly found that everything was going wrong. The *Alaska*, then the fastest ship afloat, had sailed from Liverpool on March 3 and was expected in New York on Monday, the twelfth. But on reaching Sandy Hook on the eleventh, the captain decided to wait until the weather improved. Next day, instead, it was even worse, and passengers were ordered to stay below. They were told—perhaps to allay their concern, which it did not—that since the weather was so bad on land they were better off aboard the steamer.

Even when the *Alaska* and other steamers went into port on Tuesday and Wednesday, they had to wait a day or more for tugs to clear a passage through the ice at the piers. The *Alaska*'s captain asked one of the first-class passengers, a young American doctor who spoke German and French, to go down to steerage and calm the hysterical passengers. He feared that they would get beyond control. On top of their other woes, sailors had stolen some of their valuables, especially their fur or sheepskin coats, which were often a chief part of the wealth of peasants from northern Europe. The young doctor said that after the landing, "I helped them get jobs shoveling—two dollars a day was simply colossal."

In contrast, the captain of the immigrant ship *Slavonia*, from the Baltic port of Stettin, had no such commotion to report. Asked by reporters about the storm, he shrugged. "Only the usual winter weather," he said.

"A SOMEWHAT UNUSUAL CLASS OF STORM"

"A Somewhat Unusual
Class of Storm"

PROFESSOR CLEVELAND ABBE, founder and organizer of the United States Weather Service, was the person best qualified to analyze the blizzard, now that it was over, and to explain what had been going on up there and why it had all been so inadequately predicted.

"The element that fooled us was the ocean winds, about which we never have any warning," he said. "You see, we know so little anyway, and there is so much more of which we are and must be ignorant. . . . We are utterly ignorant of what is going on to the east of us, and overhead."

Unlike the forthright Abbe, General Adolphus Greely of the Washington Weather Station did not say "we know so little." That was not an appropriate thought for the Age of Confidence. Instead, writing in the first issue of the *National Geographic*, Greely pointed out a need for telegraphic signal stations at outlying points off the coast, such as Newfoundland, Bermuda, and Nassau. These stations were shortly established, along with two at high altitudes, one on Mount Washington, in

New Hampshire, and another on Pikes Peak, in Colorado. Weather balloons, which were to change all previous thinking about the formation and structure of cyclonic storms, did not come into use for another fifty years. As for the great blizzard itself, Greely said that it belonged to "a somewhat unusual class of storm on a very grand scale."

After leaving our shores, the Blizzard of '88 zoomed across the Atlantic and arrived in northern England on Thursday, March 15. Westmorland was the county hardest hit, with sheep dying by the hundreds and seventeen trains stranded. "The American blizzard is the worst ever known," the London *Times* wrote, explaining that although the storm came from America, the word was of English origin: " 'May I be blizzered,' is a common midland expression."

The New York *Times* took umbrage. "Not without protest will Americans submit to be plundered piecemeal of any portion of that faculty of picturesque eloquence which has enriched Americanese with blizzard. The word is simply a bit of onomatopoeia. Like the hoof-beats in Virgil's poetry . . . the word is supposed to sound more or less like the thing it denotes."

The transatlantic argument went on for weeks, with a counterattack next from the Midlands to the effect that their common expression "May I be blizzered" meant that the speaker is bowled over, or knocked off his feet—like a person in a blizzard. And when, on March 19, a major storm bore down on Germany, it too was called the American Blizzard, and the news came back across the Atlantic that the word had a German origin and derived from *Blitz*.

Here at home, there was a great deal of talk about past storms and how they compared with this one. Within living memory, there had been several impressive storms: in 1845, a ten-hour snowfall had caused the collapse of a row of half-finished New York houses; another, in 1867, had halted East

River ferry traffic and given impetus to the notion of building a bridge. Two eighteenth-century storms ranked as historic: the one of 1778, during the British occupation of New York City; and another, in 1717, centering on Cape Cod. Cotton Mather had made it the subject of detailed diary entries. "The Indians near an hundred years old affirm that their Fathers never told them of anything that equalled it. . . . The Ocean was in a prodigious Ferment, and after it was over, vast heaps of little shells were driven ashore, where they were never seen before. Mighty shoals of Porpoises also kept a play day in the disturbed waves of our Harbours.

"The odd Accidents befalling many poor people whose Cottages were totally covered with the Snow, and not the very tops of the Chimneys to be seen, would afford a Story. But their not being any relation to philosophy in them, I forbear them."

On the Great Plains of the West, where, according to the American lexicographers, the word *blizzard* had originated, blizzards could occur any winter. In 1888, one had already swept across the Dakota Territory, in January. It was called the Schoolchildren's Storm, because it began while school was in session, changing a mild, sunny day to a nightmare of snow and wind. Scores of lives were lost.

In a rather bizarre effort at humor, officials of several Great Plains cities wrote to Mayor Hewitt, asking facetiously whether he needed any help:

"Huron, [South] Dakota, under a mild spring, now sends her sympathy to blizzard-stricken New York. If needed you may draw on us for $50 to relieve the storm sufferers."

And from St. Paul, Minnesota:

"Unaccustomed to storms of such severity as to cause railroad and telegraphic isolation from the outside world and never having had people frozen to death in the street, we shall be glad to contribute to any relief fund which may be started for your afflicted people. Weather here yesterday and today mild and beautiful."

The letters were published by the *Sun* under the headline DAKOTA JOKES US. The mayor was not amused. He replied with coldly courteous letters, stating that New York needed no help, but thank you very much.

Bodies were still being found during the next days and even weeks: an elderly couple discovered between their house and barn in Norwich, Connecticut; a Brooklyn lamplighter "who started out to do his work, but lighted only three lamps"; a postman; a young woman music teacher; a child with schoolbooks. On Long Island, Joseph King, a young switchman for the railroad, was near death in a snowdrift when he was found by a dog, which bit him, restoring consciousness. The dog's owner took King home, while he moaned deliriously, "Please let me go or I shall lose my job."

By Friday, March 16, more than eight hundred funerals and burials were waiting to take place in New York alone. Henry Bergh's funeral was finally held on Friday morning at St. Mark's-in-the-Bouwerie, with Mayor Hewitt as a pallbearer, along with other prominent New Yorkers. The floral tributes were far fewer than usual at an important funeral, but they included a wreath from P. T. Barnum and another adorned with a photograph of a Saint Bernard. "It was a singular coincidence," observed the Boston *Transcript*, "that the death of the most steadfast friend the horse ever had, Henry Bergh, should have occurred just at a time when these dumb animals were most in need of a friend."

An obituary appeared in Wednesday morning's newspapers for a leading New Yorker, Theodorus Van Wyck, said to have been frozen in a snowbank. On Wednesday afternoon, Mr. Van Wyck walked into the office of the *Times*, to demonstrate that the story had needed more careful checking.

During the first two weeks of April, headlines were devoted almost every day to the blizzard-induced illness of former Senator Roscoe Conkling. He had been in bed since a day or two after his long walk, and was now attended by a team of doctors who seemed unable to cure him of a severe infection of the inner right ear, complicated by pneumonia. Although he was in great pain and intermittently delirious, Conkling's vitality was astonishing, and he was a difficult patient, constantly tearing at bandages and trying to get out of bed. As a last resort, it was decided to drill a hole into his skull and drain the abscess, a risky procedure in those days. In spite of the operation—or perhaps because of it—Conkling continued to worsen, and on April 18, he died.

Five years later, a statue of the once-famous senator was erected in Madison Square. So brief is the fame of some politicians that no ceremony was held to unveil it. Today, very few passersby have any notion who Roscoe Conkling was, or that he met his fate floundering in snowdrifts on that very spot.

In the countryside, people were marooned for up to two weeks, there being no shovelers or plows to come to their rescue. "I walked over treetops," wrote a farmer "and could not tell exactly whose land I was on, as the fences were not visible." Main roads were opened by gangs of local men, using multiple yokes of oxen; but even that took days.

In the cities, the snowdrifts fast became mottled and dirty. Pedestrians were doused in slush, and the gutters ran rivers. Floods developed in upstate New York, but fortunately only in isolated places. That same week came news of 100,000 deaths in China in a flood of the Yangtse, but 100,000 Chinese deaths were hard to relate to, particularly at this hectic time.

In Manhattan, snow in backyards, which impeded the use of doors and clotheslines, had to be painstakingly packed into barrels, and carried through the house to the street, where it was eventually dealt with by the shovel brigades.

"The number and size of these gangs of shovellers," said the *Sun* "suggested the thought that the city was becoming Latinized to an extent undreamed of. But ... among them were well-dressed and comfortable-looking men, kid-gloved day laborers as it were." This phenomenon was attributed to "the stagnation of business."

One business was not stagnating. Ridley's, the store that had been burdened by a glut of twelve hundred snow shovels on the previous Saturday, had sold every one of them by the end of Blizzard Week, earning a profit of eighteen hundred dollars. Ridley's buyer, in disgrace on Saturday, received a raise.

A male-chauvinist note, from the *Sun*: "Hundreds of the ever-moving shovels were agitated by children and women. The former made up by activity for lack of strength, but the latter made a mess of it in their attacks on the huge snow piles. ... There were a great many of them to be seen, up town, down town, and all over town, but their little fire shovels and the kitchen pokers for picks were not very effectual. Another trouble was their different notion of work. A man would attack a drift with the simple purpose of dislodging it. No matter though snow remained under his feet, if the big pile was over the gutter instead of on the sidewalk, he was content. But a woman, though cleaning a spot only big enough to serve as a resting place for her dainty feet, must have that spot broom-clean and dry, or feel as though she had suffered defeat."

A blind man could have told when the city was back on its feet by listening to the sounds. Back at last came the horsecar bells, the chuffing of el locomotives, the cries of newsboys and street peddlers, the incessant din of hooves and wheels, the many-voiced horns of craft on the rivers. In telegraph offices, the usual clicking and clacking was strangely absent from Monday to Wednesday evening and, in many areas, much longer. A young telegraph operator who worked for the New York Central Railroad had remained on duty for nearly forty-eight hours, trying to send messages for Chauncey Depew. At one point on Monday he heard a faint click.

" 'That's somebody,' I said to myself. I adjusted my relay instrument and got Albany. 'What have you?' I asked the operator there. He replied: 'Nothing but snow.' Then I told him I had a message from Mr. Depew to be relayed from the Grand Central by way of Albany. I started to send it but halfway through, it stopped.

"For two days I could get nothing through by wire. Everything was chaos. The freight cars filled with provisions were still stalled at 38th Street, and the merchants were anxious to get the food. I was kept on duty trying to get messages through. Finally I succeeded and sent sixty messages in half an hour for Mr. Depew."

Seven steamers docked in New York on Wednesday, and several sailed, but without cargo. Long Island Sound steamers resumed service on Thursday. More schooners and other sailing ships came limping into port with hair-raising tales to tell. The captain of one four-masted schooner had been swept overboard by a giant wave, and then another brought him back. One of his crew was thrown over the wheel and his skull fractured, and the mate suffered serious injuries from being thrown against the forward house. The ship would have to be towed to her home port, Boston.

Off the New England coast, the crew of the schooner *W. L. White* had taken to the boats and abandoned the ship. With no one at the helm she voyaged for nearly a year. For some time she tossed about in the Gulf Stream, a collision danger for transatlantic ships. At last, after covering more than five thousand miles, she stranded in the Hebrides.

Another schooner, the *James Ford*, bound from Baltimore to New Bedford, was wallowing helplessly, eight feet of water in her hold, when a bark came to the rescue and took off the crew. According to one of them, "The boat had hardly got back when the last of the *James Ford* was seen. She gave a weak sort of a kick and a struggle and took a dive to Davey Jones's locker, head first."

At the Seawanhaka Corinthian Yacht Club, at Oyster Bay, Long Island, members looked in vain for the yacht *Cythera*. After weeks and months of expiring hope, the boat and all aboard were adjudged "probably lost." *The American Yachtsman*, for June 1888, declared these men to have been "as brave and skilful yachtsmen as ever trod the deck of any yacht. . . . What yacht could have passed through this ordeal unscathed? None."

One did, however. The *Iroquois*, from Boston, sighted on Saturday by Inglis and his shipmates on the *Colt*, arrived at her destination in Florida, not unscathed, but still sailing.

Mayor Abram Hewitt, who had campaigned on promises of reform and improvement for New York City, had tried as recently as February to get a subway bill through the legislature, but without success. From the mayor's point of view, the Great Blizzard had come along at the right time and place. No sooner had the els, trains, and horsecars succumbed to the storm than every newspaper ran mordant editorials on the deficiencies of the city's transportation and communication systems. "An underground rapid transit system would have done what the elevated roads could not do," commented the *Times*. "If the telegraph wires had been placed underground as contemplated by the law, they would have been made to subserve a specially important duty at a time when they were most sorely needed. . . . stilled railways and surface telegraphic communication will no longer answer for this great city." The storm "demonstrated the inadequacy of the elevated railroad system to such an emergency. . . . [it is] intolerable that the internal transit of New York should be at the mercy of the elements. The ordinary business of the elevated roads has far outgrown their capacity, while they cannot even pretend to cope with great emergencies."

On March 18, the *Times* came up with its own plan for a subway that would run from the Battery all the way to the north end of Manhattan. All along the route, "owners would welcome it," because it would lead to neighborhood improvements. The trains would have electric motors and electric lights, and receive ventilation through air shafts. (This plan, very much as set forth, was to come to fruition some fifteen years later.)

The problem of overhead wires was just as serious. Some wires were already underground, and the conduits were there, but the companies—telegraph, telephone, and electric—found wires on poles to be cheaper and easier to repair. Although the telephone company's poles and wires fared better in the blizzard than the others, telegraph and electric wires and poles often fell upon them and brought them down, too. Subscribers could sometimes get through to the hello girl, but seldom to the party they were calling. A few long-distance lines faithfully gave service to Poughkeepsie, but that was not much comfort for those who wanted to talk to Washington or New Haven.

Each utility had its own poles. Those of the five electric companies were five stories high, and a few poles were nearly twice as tall. The poles carrying arc lights in Union Square reached upward 150 feet. Single poles could carry between 100 and 200 wires, and there were thousands of wires, running in all directions. Firemen trying to do their jobs were often in danger of electrocution. Two years previously, the legislature had passed stern laws in regard to wires: they were *all* to be taken down and buried. But the companies had been blandly ignoring the law, despite the fulminations of Hewitt and the newspapers.

On January 1, 1889, Abram Hewitt was succeeded as Mayor by Hugh J. Grant, another reformer. One of Grant's first acts in office concerned the wires: those already up must be removed and placed underground within ninety days, he decreed, or they would be torn down. To erect any more was forbidden. "When we fix a time we mean it," said Grant. "When the time is ended the poles will come down."

The telephone company, while all in favor of putting wires underground, objected that there was no satisfactory way of doing it. There was only a system that had been tried in Philadelphia and failed—"since it was blowing up every little while because of unavoidable accumulation of gas and inevitable destruction of insulation on the wires." However, seeing that Grant meant business, the telephone people suddenly found a special copper sheathing in which the wires could be buried. It cost more, but it solved the problem.

When, at the end of ninety days, the city moved to chop down the utility poles, Jay Gould, who was an owner of Western Union, cried "unconstitutional" and obtained a court injunction. However, within two weeks the court empowered the city to go ahead with its plans. In mid-April 1889, the poles began to fall like forest oaks, and wires were rolled up and taken away. Crowds followed the workmen and cheered and cried "Timber!" as the poles hit the ground. Gould and the other owners then tried to reclaim the wire, but, since they had not obeyed the mayor, they were sternly prevented from doing so. At last the city could see the sky again, and after a few hectic months of digging and laying cables, the main job was done.

In the end, the new system proved to be cheaper for the utility companies.

Now that the storm was over, ministers, philosophers, editors, and amateur poets were all expressing themselves. What did it mean? What was it all about?

"Talk about a blizzard—/ One of the worst ever known,/ You need not go out West,/ We have had one of our own," wrote an agitated poet to the New Haven *Register*. The rector of Trinity Church in New Haven took as his Sunday sermon text Psalm 51: "Wash me and I shall be whiter than snow." Said he, "This section of the country has just passed through a strange experience . . . The discoveries of an advanced civilization have been powerless. Businessmen have been isolated and to a certain extent idle. Communications between cities have been severed. It has been a wonderful experience to live through to remember and hereafter relate." It all had reminded him of his vacation in the Alps, and he wound up his sermon with a travel talk. Perhaps it was the best thing to do, since he was plainly unable to explain what the Lord had been up to. Even those who had not suffered were in shock, and they needed to be lured away from anxiety and back to confidence.

Another clergyman cheered his flock with a little clairvoyance: "In the next century when people travel in aerial cars there will be no blockades. I am very positive science will accomplish this wonderful method of travel before the millennium comes."

Most newspaper editors saw some ironic messages in the blizzard experience. The Springfield *Republican* opined that "The cruelty of the elements is as nothing in comparison with that of man to man. But what are these lives lost in comparison with those which a single great battle in our last war, or the next European war, dispatched or will slaughter?"

But perhaps the editorial that best fitted the general feeling of the public was the Hartford *Courant*'s: "It is the boasting and progressive Nineteenth Century that is paralyzed, while the slowgoing Eighteenth would have taken such an experience without a ruffle. It is our own 'advantages' that have gone back on us.

"You can get your beef by rail from Chicago in two day's time or so; it is cheaper to buy of a milkman than to keep a cow; stores deliver, and so often, free of charge, that a day's supply is a household's provisioning . . . Three miles from work is really the same as close by . . . many people can live in one town and work in another . . . traveling in ease, even luxury. The telegraph will flash a thought a thousand miles for us.

"But lo . . . there comes a storm . . . there is no railroad, no telegraph, no horse car, no milk, no delivery of food at the door. We starve in the midst of plenty. . . . and the telephone, sole survivor in the wreck of our superior 'advantages' plays the amusing part of mockery and enables people to tell each other that they can't meet and storekeepers to assure housekeepers that they cannot give them what they need. This is a questionable triumph of latter-day invention. It warns us to be discreet and temperate in our boasting. . . . It is only a snowstorm, but it has downed us."

A very small newspaper, the *Transcript* of Holyoke, Massachusetts, ventured a prediction. For years to come, it said, people would "look back upon this March snowstorm as unrivaled, unapproachable, unique and ideal." And after forty or fifty years had passed, the prediction was proved correct. Men and women who had lived through the blizzard, even those who had had frightening experiences, looked back on it with a curious nostalgia. Members of the Society of Blizzard Men and

Blizzard Ladies remembered it as "a great communal adventure." Said one of them, "It had its tragic side but curiously left in its wake mainly good will, and to its survivors it has become almost a household symbol standing not only for the storm itself but also for all that was best in the 'good old days.' " And another confessed, "We blizzard survivors are not only organizing to keep alive the traditions of the storm but we are sick and tired of all this modernity and want to go back to the days when we New Yorkers lived simply and got our fun out of simple things."

As we have seen, the good old days included a considerable admixture of unpleasantness, and the "great communal adventure" was a nightmare to many. Perhaps what these Blizzard Men and Ladies were really nostalgic for was the unabashed optimism of the Age of Confidence.

On March 20, 1888, the editorial offices of Wilmington's leading newspaper, *Every Evening*, received a return visit from John Cooper, who had stopped in on March 10 to tell them that his cherry tree was about to bloom. This time he brought along two large branches in full blossom. He said the tree had continued its customary springtime budding all through the days of the blizzard, and no sooner had the sun come out than the buds had burst into flower.

"First again," he said. "Just like it always is."

He didn't even seem surprised.

Appendix

From the official records of the New York Weather Station:

Monday, March 12: Rain changed to snow at 12:10 A.M. 10″ on ground at 7:00 A.M.; 15.5″ by 3:00 P.M.; another 1″ fell before midnight. Barometer reached low of 29.21″ at 10:00 A.M., commenced very slow rise at 1:00 P.M. Total day's fall, 16.5″.

Maximum temperature, 34.9°; minimum 10.7°. Wind speed, 48 mph maximum; 32.8 mph average; from northwest, then west.

Tuesday, March 13: Light snow ended at 5:55 A.M. Resumed at 1:55 P.M., ended at 7:05 P.M. Flurries later. Total day's fall, 3.0″.

7:00 A.M.: temperature, 6°; wind, west at 37 mph
3:00 P.M.: temperature, 12°; wind, west at 39 mph
10:00 P.M.: temperature, 14°; wind, west at 30 mph

At 7 A.M. the storm was centered over Narragansett Bay. At 10 P.M. the center was near New London and beginning to lose intensity.

APPENDIX

Wednesday, March 14: Light snow ended at 3:40 A.M. Resumed 6:25 A.M. to 7:15 A.M. and 10:40 A.M. to 2:50 P.M. Total day's fall, 1.4″.

Three-day storm total: 20.9″
7:00 A.M.: temperature, 23°; wind, northwest at 14 mph
3:00 P.M.: temperature, 39°; wind, north at 13 mph
10:00 P.M.: temperature, 34°; wind, northwest at 12 mph

Bibliography

The best sources for this book were the more than twelve hundred letters of reminiscence, written in the 1930s and later, by members of the Society of Blizzard Men and Blizzard Ladies. These are in the manuscript collection of the New-York Historical Society.

BOOKS, REPORTS, AND PAPERS

Adams, Charles Francis. *Railroads: Their Origins and Problems*. Reprint. New York: Harper and Row, 1969.

Alexander, William. *The New Equitable Building*. New York: privately printed, 1887.

Annual Report of the Operations of the United States Life-Saving Service. Washington: Government Printing Office, 1898.

Bennett, Commander Robert F. *The Life-Saving Service at Sandy Hook Station, 1854–1915*. Washington: U.S. Coast Guard Historical Monograph Program, 1976.

Best, Gerald M. *Snowplow*. Berkeley: Howell-North Books, 1966.

Brigham, Johnson. "Blaine, Conkling and Garfield." Paper read before the Prairie Club of Des Moines, April 10, 1915.

BIBLIOGRAPHY

Burnham, Alan. *New York Landmarks*. Middletown, Conn.: Municipal Art Society of New York and Wesleyan University Press, 1961.

Campbell, Mrs. Helen. *Darkness and Daylight*. Hartford: The Hartford Publishing Co., 1895.

Chidsey, D. B. *The Gentleman from New York: A Life of Roscoe Conkling*. New Haven: Yale University Press, 1935.

The City of New York, A Complete Guide. New York: Taintor Brothers, 1885.

Club Book of the Seawanhaka Corinthian Yacht Club. New York: E. F. Weeks, 1904.

Cochoran, Thomas C. *Railroad Leaders, 1845–1890*. New York: Russell and Russell, 1953.

Coleman, Marion Moore. *Fair Rosalind: The American Career of Helena Modjeska*. Cheshire, Conn.: Cherry Hill Books, 1969.

Collins, Frederick L. *Money Town*. New York: G. P. Putnam's Sons, 1946.

Covello, Leonard. *The Heart Is the Teacher*. New York: McGraw Hill, 1958.

Cudahy, Brian J. *Under the Sidewalks of New York*. Brattleboro, Vermont: Stephen Greene Press, 1979.

Daley, Robert. *The World Beneath the City*. Philadelphia: J. B. Lippincott, Co., 1959.

Delany, Edmund T. *Greenwich Village*. Barre, Mass.: Barre Publishers, 1968.

Depew, Chauncey. *My Memories of Eighty Years*. New York: Charles Scribner's Sons, 1922.

Durso, Joseph. *Madison Square Garden*. New York: Simon and Schuster, 1979.

An Examination of the Subject of Street Cleaning in the City of New York, made at the Request of Hon. Hugh J. Grant, Mayor. New York: Department of Street Cleaning, 1891.

Frisinger, H. Howard. *The History of Meteorology to 1800*. Historical Monograph Series, American Meteorological Society. New York: Science History Publications, 1977.

Gerard, James W. *The Impress of Nationalities Upon the City of New York*. New York: Columbia Spectator Publishing Co., 1883.

Graham, Robert. *New York and Its Masters*. New York: Church Temperance Society, 1887.

Greely, Gen. Adolphus W. *American Weather*. New York: Dodd, Mead and Co., 1888.

Griswold, Wesley S. *Train Wreck!* Brattleboro, Vt.: The Stephen Greene Press, 1969.

BIBLIOGRAPHY

Harlow, Alvin F. *Old Bowery Days*. New York and London: D. Appleton and Co., 1931.

Hobbs, Charles H. *Illustrated Guide to New York City*. New York: Charles H. Hobbs and Co., 1889.

Hungerford, Edward. *The Story of Public Utilities*. New York: G. P. Putnam's Sons, 1928.

Jennings, N. A., and McC. Lingan. *New York in the Blizzard*. New York: Rogers and Sherwood, 1888.

Jensen, Oliver. *American Heritage History of the Railroads of America*. New York: American Heritage Publishing Co., 1975.

Kennedy, Susan E. *If All We Did Was to Weep at Home*. Bloomington, Ind. and London: Indiana University Press, 1979.

Kenney, Thomas and Peter Standford. *South Street Around 1900*. New York: South Street Seaport Museum, 1970.

Kimball, Sumner I. *Organization and Methods of the U.S. Life-Saving Service*. Washington: Government Printing Office, 1912.

King, Moses. *King's Views of the New York Stock Exchange*. New York: King's Handbooks, 1898.

Laughton, L. G. C. *Great Storms*. New York: William Farquahar Payson, 1931.

Leonard, John William. *History of the City of New York*. New York: Journal of Commerce and Commercial Bulletin, 1910.

Ludlum, David. *Early American Winters*. Boston: American Meteorological Society, 1966.

———. *The American Weather Book*. Boston: Houghton Mifflin Co., 1982.

———. *The New Jersey Weather Book*. Boston: Houghton Mifflin Co., 1982.

Marcus, Benjamin. *A Historical Sketch of Madison Square*. New York: Meriden Monographs No. 1, 1894.

Miller, John Andrew. *Fares, Please!* New York: Dover, 1960.

Moody, John. *The Railroad Builders*. New Haven: Yale University Press, 1920.

Nevins, Allan. *Abram S. Hewitt*. New York: Harper and Brothers, 1935.

———. *The Emergence of Modern America, 1865–1878*. (Vol. 8 in a History of American Life). New York: The Macmillan Co., 1927.

O'Gara W. H. *In All Its Fury*. Lincoln, Neb.: Union College Press, 1947.

Opinion of the Medical Profession on the Condition and Needs of the City of New York in Regard to Street-cleaning. New York: Trow's Printing Co., 1881.

Phelps, M. N. *Kate Chase, Dominant Daughter*. New York: Thomas Y. Crowell Co., 1935.

BIBLIOGRAPHY

Pilot Lore. New York: United New York and New Jersey Sandy Hook Pilots Benevolent Association, 1922.

Rayne, Martha L. *What Can a Woman Do?* Petersburgh, N.Y.: Eagle Publication Co., 1893.

Report and Proceedings of the Senate Committee Appointed to Investigate the Police Department of the City of New York. Albany, N.Y.: James B. Lyon, 1895 (5 volumes).

Richardson, James F. *The New York Police.* New York: Oxford University Press, 1970.

Riis, Jacob A. *Children of the Poor.* Reprint. New York and London: Johnson Corporation, 1970.

Russell, Charles Edward. *From Sandy Hook to 62°.* New York: Century Co., 1929.

Ryan, Mary P. *Womanhood in America.* New York: Franklin Watts, 1983.

Shaw, Robert B. *A History of Railroad Accidents, Safety Precautions and Operating Practices.* Potsdam, New York: Clarkson College of Technology, 1978.

Smith, Alfred E. *Up to Now, An Autobiography.* New York: Viking Press, 1929.

Snow, Edward Rowe. *Great Gales and Dire Disasters.* New York: Dodd, Mead and Co., 1952.

Steele, Zulma. *Angel in Top Hat.* New York: Harper and Brothers, 1942.

Stilgoe, John R. *Metropolitan Corridor.* New Haven: Yale University Press, 1983.

Strong, Samuel Meredith. *The Great Blizzard of 1888.* New York: privately printed arrangement by Marion Overton. Brooklyn, 1938.

Sutton, Felix. *The Big Show.* New York: Doubleday and Co., 1971.

Todd, A. L. *Abandoned, the Story of the Greely Arctic Expedition, 1881–1884.* New York: McGraw-Hill, 1961.

Tolman, Dr. William H., and Charles Hemstreet. *The Better New York.* New York: The Baker and Taylor Co., 1904.

Van Pelt, Daniel. *Leslie's History of the Greater New York.* 3 vols. New York: Arkell Publishing Co., 1898.

Van Wyck, Frederick. *Recollections of an Old New Yorker.* New York: Liveright, Inc., 1932.

Ventresca, Francesco. *Personal Reminiscences of a Naturalized American.* New York: Daniel Ryerson, Inc., 1937.

Werner, W. R. *Barnum.* New York: Harcourt, Brace and Co., 1923.

Werstein, Irving. *The Blizzard of '88.* New York: Thomas Y. Crowell Co., 1960.

BIBLIOGRAPHY

Whitman, Walt. *Daybooks and Notebooks*. Edited by William White. Vol. 2., New York: New York University Press, 1978.

Wilkerson, James A., ed. *Hypothermia, Frostbite and Other Cold Injuries*. Seattle: The Mountaineers, 1986.

WPA Writers Program. *A Maritime History of New York*. Reprint. New York: Haskell House Publishers, Ltd., 1975.

ARTICLES

Chittenden, L. E. "The Rapid Transit Problem in New York City." *Harper's Weekly* 35 (February 21, 1891).

Clark, Gen. Emmons. "Street Cleaning in Large Cities." *Popular Science Monthly* 38 (April 1891).

——. "Sanitary Improvement in New York During the Last Quarter of a Century." *Popular Science Monthly* 39 (June 1891).

Copley, Frank Barclay. "The Measure of Human Grit." *American Magazine* 71 (December 1910; January and February 1911).

"Destruction of Electric Wires by a Snow Storm." *Scientific American* 64 (February 7, 1891).

Elsing, W. T. "Life in New York Tenement Houses." *Scribners* 11 (June 1892).

"Extension of Rapid Transit Facilities in New York City." *Scientific American* 67 (December 3, 1891).

Fawcett, E. "Woes of the New York Working Girl." *Arena* 5 (December 1891).

Ferris, G. I. "How a Great City Is Fed." *Harper's Weekly* 34 (March 22, 1890).

Greely, Gen. A. W. "The Great Storm of March 11–14, 1888." *National Geographic* 1 (May 1888).

Humphreys, M. G. "The People's Four-in-Hand: the Fifth Avenue Bus." *Harper's Weekly* 35 (July 11, 1891).

Kelley F. "Decade of Retrogression." *Arena* 4 (August 1891).

Milliken, D. "Street Obstructions in New York." *Harper's Weekly* 36 (January 16, 1892).

Straus, W. "How the New York Deathrate Was Reduced by Opening Six Milk Depots." *Forum* 18 (November 1894).

Waring, G. E. "Some Changes in the Streets of New York." *Harper's Weekly* 39 (June 22, 1895).

BIBLIOGRAPHY

Wright, A. W. "Seeing the Metropolis Grow." *Harper's Weekly* 34 (February 1, 1890).

NEWSPAPERS

The following newspapers reporting on the blizzard were also very useful:

Albany *Journal*
Boston *Transcript*
Hartford *Courant*
Holyoke *Transcript*
Meriden *Journal*
Narragansett *Times*
New Haven *Journal Courier*
New Haven *Register*
New York *Times*

New York *Sun*
New York *World*
Philadelphia *Bulletin*
Providence *Journal*
Springfield *Republican*
Washington *Post*
Washington *Star*
Wilmington *Every Evening*

MARY CABLE was born in Cleveland, Ohio, and brought up in Providence, Rhode Island. After a number of years in New York and in various foreign countries, she now lives in Santa Fe, New Mexico.

A recipient of grants from both the National Endowment for the Arts and the National Endowment for the Humanities, she has written several books on various aspects of American social history, including *Lost New Orleans* and *Top Drawer*. She has also served as an editor/writer for a number of publications including *The New Yorker, Harper's Bazaar, American Heritage,* and *Horizon*.

The Blizzard of '88 is her tenth book.